A SENSE OF HISTORY

John S. Hatcher

A SENSE OF HISTORY

A Collection of Poems

Illustrated by Jill Hatcher

GEORGE RONALD

OXFORD

GEORGE RONALD, Publisher
46 HIGH STREET, KIDLINGTON, OXFORD, OX5 2DN
© JOHN S. HATCHER 1990
All Rights Reserved

British Library Cataloguing in Publication Data

Hatcher, John S.
A sense of history: a collection of poems
I Title
811.54

ISBN 0–85398–312–7
ISBN 0–85398–313–5 pbk

Typeset by Photoprint, Torquay, Devon
Printed and bound in Great Britain by
Billing & Sons Ltd, Worcester

for
John Albert Hatcher
Jill Hatcher
Helen Grace Hatcher
James Varqá Hatcher

The best work I leave behind

Acknowledgements

In addition to my wife Lucia, whose opinion I value above all others, and those who through the years have encouraged me to continue with my poetry, I would like to express my appreciation to my colleagues at the University of South Florida who saw fit to award me a sabbatical for this project. Without that release from my teaching duties, this volume would in no wise have been possible.

The art work in this book is all based on photographs from family albums, except for the portrait of Varqá and Rúḥu'lláh on page 162. The original photograph comes from the Bahá'í World Centre.

Contents

PART SEVEN

TUNNEL VISION

PART EIGHT

WAITING FOR AMERICA

PART NINE

A SENSE OF HISTORY

ix

Foreword

IN the early 1600s my ancestors emigrated from England to Henrico County, Virginia. From 1644 to 1659 William Hatcher was a member of the House of Burgesses in Colonial Virginia, something my aunt Cynthia, a hard-working school teacher in Franklin, Tennessee, took great pride in. Of course, we do not have to look back more than a generation or so to discover how we are all a hybrid of incalculable influences, most beyond our understanding and all quite beyond our control. Nevertheless, as Faulkner noted in his 1949 Nobel Prize acceptance speech, it is part of the poet's task to delve into history, not only to understand the motive force that brought us to our present circumstances, but to help us discern in that recollected past the future hope latent in the tangle of our lives:

> It is his privilege to help man endure by lifting his heart, by reminding him of the courage and honor and hope and pride and compassion and pity and sacrifice which have been the glory of his past. The poet's voice need not merely be the record of man, it can be one of the props, the pillars to help him endure and prevail.

These poems are about history, personal and otherwise. Some are history itself in the raw and some are painted thickly with reference to particular times and events. I have provided the reader a sufficiency of notes to uncover these allusions because it is not the fact of history that interests me, but the sense of it.

John S. Hatcher
1990

Theories of History

Historians are for the most part very scholarly men nowadays; they go in fear rather of small errors than of disconnectedness; they dread the certain ridicule of a wrong date more than the disputable attribution of a wrong value . . .

H.G. Wells

EVOLUTION

All men have been created to carry forward an ever-advancing civilization.

Bahá'u'lláh

a molten seed
spun off from stars,
balanced perfectly between
willful centrifugality
and the warming love
of Newton's sun,

cools
while in murky recesses
of bubbling pools
percolates natural law
commingled with
divine plan

so that the special one
not doing well in water
is gently urged
toward the warring shore
on incipient toes
to be taught by degrees
how a thumb can work
in brilliant opposition.

INHERITANCE

Poor Hera diminished by a verdict
from the unknown shepherd boy,
sought vengeance—
the devastation of Priam's house,
of Hector whom we all loved,
of his kindred, our fathers.
Do we dare even now rebuild
what loosed passion has destroyed
or yet weaves the implacable shrew
devious threads of automatic doom
for the descended race of Ilion?

ARIADNE'S COMPLAINT

Passions create in the heart of man such turbulence that there is no longer possible to him the quiet mind on which happiness is conditioned.

Lily B. Campbell

It was my mother
who did it,
couldn't get
her fill,

gave birth to
a degenerate
that annually
made beasts of us;

unnatural, socially
unacceptable
(bad hygiene);
now I

wait in the sand
on this forgotten beach—
forsaken, violated,
tricked;

don't tell me
parental sins
aren't visited on
the kids.

THE BRAIDED ROPE
for Kwan Jang Nim Yung Ho Jun

On a tumulus from the Kogooryo reign
two men wait eternally for a move
to signal a studied response.

In Seokkooram cave in Kyongjoo
the mighty Silla warrior Keumgang
blocks high, blocks low—

Sonnal-Keumgang-Makki
as I do now the same
like Hwarang before me.

Each of us perpetually
student then teacher,
father and son forever.

Beside dim lantern light
Yi Deokmoo labored into the dawn
remembering, remembering,

the angle of arm and leg,
the hands like knives,
the heel like a hammer,

the curve between forefinger and thumb—
Ageum-Son to the throat,
the deadly Tiger-Mouth.

But first there must be *Do*,
the path of choices
each seeks himself.

Where there is no choosing,
there can be no *Do*,
only the moment's chimera.

Each becomes strong
to give strength away,
equal hearts bound by the common good.

We are mirrors
facing mirrors,
effacing our own image.

Behold the rice plant:
those stalks stooping near to the earth
like reverent wise old men

bend under the weight
of their own fullness;
the empty shafts stand tall.

Now you, a flowering branch,
think to thrive
apart from the tree?

If you wither to grey ash
at your master's gnarled feet,
you will grasp too late

the point of balance between
your own cunning path up Taebek
and surrender to the ancestral way,

a cord stretching back before
Yi Deokmoo's memory,
reaching forward beyond the sweep

of even your young eyes,
like the braided strands of this rope
with which I test your confident hands,

and which you cannot sunder
so long as diminutive threads
remain entwined—

at one end anchored to ageless generations
whose wisdom makes you wise;
at the other end, a mountain you must ascend.

FOREKNOWLEDGE AND THE TRUE STORY OF MARVIN RAINWATER'S REMARKABLE VISION

Remember Marvin Rainwater,
Arthur Godfrey's friendly Indian
who sang a lot like Eddie Arnold?

he showed up three days ago
barely recognizable
and he reminded me

    of Demodocus,
the old Phaeacian bard
who whispered
after the courtiers
left the hearth
and Ulysses lay exhausted
asleep on his fur bed
dreaming of the young Nausicaa

    not the distant Penelope
or the recent Circe
or Calypso of yesterday
but the lithe and present
                Nausicaa

chasing her ball
into the bushes
white-armed after bathing
and rubbing herself
with aromatic oils;

blind though he was,
Demodocus knew
that the stranger wanted
more than a hitchhike

    back to Ithaca
with its tedium
of the king's per diem
back to the ever-faithful
ever-constant
ever-beyond-his-understanding
Penelope.

Demodocus could see it all—
the wornout histories
were for the court,
the future he saved for himself
alone at night
strumming of things to come:

the ultimate boredom
generating the ultimate gesture—
a Sunday jaunt past
the Pillars of Hercules,
that boisterous laugh
bouncing off the rock cliffs.

And Marvin?
well, he knew it all too!
Not Tony Marvin
not Julius La Rosa
not Hali Loki or Carmel Quin.
None of the other little Godfreys
had the slightest idea.
Only Marvin knew because
only he was an Indian.

Marvin saw
and left the doomed enterprise
and I, my dear,
who am a gypsy,
leave Tuesday
for New Zealand

but don't get nervous—
I'm just a half-breed.

MEDITATIONS AT A PERFORMANCE OF THE GUARNERI STRING QUARTET
for Joseph Bentley (1932–1988)

Just as my fingers on these keys
Make music, so the selfsame sounds
On my spirit make a music, too.
Wallace Stevens

I

Giuseppe tooled the choicest wood,
a craft passed down
from Stradivari to Uncle Andrea.

Grains of wood he knew
as lovers know
the curve of neck or turn of waist.

He labored not for the eye;
he listened until he heard
exactly what the wood might say,

bathed sap on the violin belly
to make the timbre mellow
like his mother's voice

or the sherry he sipped
at his favorite tavern
in the heart of Genoa.

With thumb and finger he could
feel the width of back
more finely than calipers,

said the tone was there
before the tree was cut,
but it spoke to him only.

His instrument hands
shaped the sound post
precisely thin;

secret lacquers he applied
layer upon layer,
a subtle sheen that glows

like living lovers' skin,
the mirror of an age,
of an idea.

2

Johannes Brahms' string quartet

After the French merchant had lent Paganini
the priceless gift—Giuseppe del Gesú's voice—
he could not in good conscience retrieve it
only to have it encased again in his foyer
to tease some envious and frivolous friends.

Niccoló enthralled Vienna
with his twenty-four *Capricci*,
the strains of which would coax
the instrument of Brahms' capacious soul.

3

Beethoven's Grosse Fuge, Opus 133, in B flat Major

From Haydn, from Mozart, Ludwig learned
until the silence of outer ear
orphaned him to pure Platonic form

where perfect counterpoint and voices like sirens
screamed out in the solitary cave of his own music—
bereft him mainly of critics' solicitude,

of rattling carriage wheels on cobbled streets,
until he discovered there in his exquisite loneliness
symphonies chambered in the genius of his brain,

and he wrested from his fright and pain
the flightful harangue he heard,
transposed a garish din of thought

into four parts barely resolved—
'Too much for our ears!' said Artaria to Holz.
Alone, ill, Ludwig with reticence agreed

the fugue an affront to the human need
for dénouement, and not exactly
what Prince Galitzin had in mind.

Only now do we hear it as it should be,
as bewildering atonal finale
to stupefy and hearken

not to elegance, the *de rigueur*;
to warn of what is upon us,
and what is soon to come.

4

Bartók, String Quartet No. 6 (1939)

Leaving his mother's side,
Béla was off to the country to hear his peasants
after years alone in their private forests

probing the dark rich earth,
their hands and fingers wrinkled, leathery,
and in their throats, arias

melodic lines the spheres themselves
reverberate at night when the stock are sleeping
and a solitary farmer treads under stars

away from even the simple house to hear
some rapturous cry pulse out from meta space
to syncopate his untrammeled heart.

Bartók heard it too, echoed in their songs,
felt the proximity of music to the human condition
as onomatopoeia befits a flash of joy.

Their measures refracted through Bartók's thought,
and taut strings, trembled over
that irreplaceable wood the notes

that here are quavering for us,
(never for the indurate tyrant)
beseeching us to lament what is irretrievable—

our misspent youth,
the love we almost won,
the iniquity we might have quenched.

<h1 style="text-align:center">5</h1>

How these deft and eloquent hands
make sensual Paganini's unbridled joy,
Ludwig's solitude, Béla's native pride.

Hear them now caress Guarneri's sacred wood,
and note their love of craftsman and the craft.
Can you hear their own music, too?

One fears what doctors will report;
One grieves for a departed friend;
another delights in the fragrance of gardenias;

The fourth feels through trilling strings,
his chin held tight against the hollow wood,
he understands exactly what the music means.

I fumble for this pen to note
the astounding confluence that is art,
this ephemeral marriage of craft and thought,

this brief and matchless juncture of our lives
of all our tuneful histories
played out so existentially.

PROGRESSIVE REVELATION AND THE PROBLEM OF FREE WILL

In the Bayán the Báb says that every religion of the past was fit to become universal. The only reason why they failed to attain that mark was the incompetence of their followers.

Shoghi Effendi

'O Jerusalem, Jerusalem,'
Christ rebuked the gathering Pharisees,
'Killing the prophets and stoning
those who are sent to you!

'How often would I
have gathered your children together
as a hen gathers her brood under her wings,
and ye would not!'

But even the ingenuous desciples,
rapt with the fire of the love they loved
could not guess how manna in the wilderness
and the unleavened loaf they broke
at that last passover feast
were the self-same bread
come down for them from heaven.

Some irony they could understand,
how Barabbas would live
and He whose only sin
was goading ritualized hearts
should be posted as a mantic sign.

Rapture of faith they had,
the bliss of thoughtless wonderment,
but the quaking earth would crack
even the rock among them.

'Show us the Father', Philip asked,
'and we shall be satisfied.'

What could He say to them then,
that to see Him was sufficient,
not as fleshly essence
but perfectly allegorized,
God's reflection and yet not God?

But he had labored with them,
had prayed, healed, taught,
and so knew in his flawless heart
they would in the end miss the point,
how he conducted this endless music
that was not his own—
motive, word, authority,
none of these his own.

Deify if you must
the words that pour from my mouth
like liquid crystal
but for the sake of God
let the body lie in peace!

'I am the true vine,
and my Father is the husbandman!'

Clear? Yes, yes,
the subordination is plain enough.

'Take this wine and drink it.
Take this bread and eat.
Now are you nourished in full,
have within your veins
the elixir that flowed
from the fountain heart
of Abraham, of Moses,
of your fathers before you.'

They feast and throb with a heat
that could melt even the iron law,
but their eyes are blank still,

and in the agony of omniscience,
He foresees a mutilation more drear
than the fatal cross he must bear,
more deep and everlasting
than nails hammered quickly into flesh.

Suddenly, even as they eat,
the bread turns waxen in their mouths,
becomes the very flesh of God!
The wine congeals into God's blood,
and then, and then at last,
becomes the Prophet's tears.

GULL FEEDING

Look ye not upon the fewness of thy numbers, rather seek ye out hearts that are pure. One consecrated soul is preferable to a thousand other souls.
'Abdu'l-Bahá

A snake file
    whipping in currents
        pausing like planes

before attack
    gulls await in turn
        the propitious motion

wrist snap thrust,
    quick bread piece
        shot skyward

slowing,
    stopping
        as on a shelf

long enough
    to
        snatch it!

All perform
    but one
        novice

impatient
    unritualized
        promethic

he breaks ranks
    descends
        towards

the feeding hand
    plucks skin, and
        dough together

Beaked heads
    click
        in unison

inside brittle
    eggshell
        skulls

ganglionic
    patterns
        shatter

a crash
    of feathers
        flash

the sun.

PART TWO
Songs of the Tollund Man

Now and then a king's thane
a vaunted warrior mindful of songs,
he who of the old legends
many recalled, a new story told
in well linked words
           Beowulf II. 867b–881a

Quid Hinieldus cum Christo?
                    Alcuin

THE TOLLUND MAN:
A DEFINITION OF THE SOUL

*The dead man who lay there was two thousand years old. A few hours earlier he
had been brought out from the sheltering peat by two men . . . As they worked,
they suddenly saw in the peatlayer a face so fresh they could only suppose they had
stumbled on a recent murder.*

P.V. Glob

Now you have reached me
may brush if you wish
the caked clay from my
thin trimmed moustache—
you are too late.

For two thousand years
I lay here entrenched
in this peat bog
waiting in a fetal pose
for redemption,

pegged down, listening
for the crunch of sod—
horse's molars munching oats,
a cold steel spade sliding
ever closer.

I was strangely calm
at the morning rite,
hands cupping the mystic brew
of finest grain from our
mostly barren fields;

As I sipped the holy potion,
swallowed hard, I stared boldly
at those blank-faced elders;
yes, the year had gone bad again—
no matter that it always did.

The priest chanted in somber tones
how mother earth would be bribed,
that special fire in his aged eyes
reflecting scintillas
of ancestral faith;

From behind a quick loop
snapped my neck rope tight,
the bowl floated from my hands;
the marsh faded as I
marveled at the public good.

After they lashed me down
sacrificially in the sacred swamp
I waited expectantly for
the mud-wife goddess to claim me
from my solitude.

Piety flowed through my veins,
gave way to passion
for her lusty arms,
her nibbling lips—
she never came.

Centuries I waited
while nations raged;
kings thundered my tomb;
the sighs of grieving wives
infested my stone sleep.

Little at a time I turned
as winter by winter
peasants sliced away
the congealing bogs
to warm their crude thatched huts.

Now you have come,
but too late to save me
though my cap is in place;
tediously pick earth from my ears—
I cannot hear you;

carve me out if you like
to warm your hearth
some hoary night;
preserve me in wine,
encase me in glass;

display me for your
snickering children
on their forced marches
through time,

some miracle the earth has wrought,
their hope of immortality,
then lift a lid
to show what's missing.

THE OLD MARINER
ca. 9th century AD

A true song I may sing of myself
of my times of rough toil on the sea
how I often endured days of drudgery,
and bitter grief consumed my soul.

On many a ship I came to know
the direst dwelling on stark rolling waves,
kept dread night watch at the prow
as the craft tossed beside rocky ledges.

Then gelid wind seized my feet
froze them in icy bonds
while sorrows pulsed hot round my heart
and hunger slit my sea-weary mind.

He who dwells on the fair land
knows not how I was worn to a sigh,
spent my winters on the ice-cold sea,
bereft of close kin on the path of exile.

Hung round with icicles
while hail swirled around me in showers,
I heard naught but the sea's roar,
the crashing of the cold grey waves.

At times the swan's song was my sole companion,
the gannet's call or the curlew's cry
in place of the laughter of men,
the gull's scream instead of honey-mead.

When savage storms battered sharp stony cliffs,
the tern or eagle screamed answers with icy feathers—
there was no giver of rings
to console my anguished heart.

He who owns ease of life on land,
who lives in quaint villages, proud and winegay,
who has not sailed on such treacherous voyages,
knows not how I dwelt on the weary sea-path.

The dark shadows come now;
snow blows from the north and frost binds the sod
while hail pelts the pleasant plains like savage grain.
Soon my soul's thoughts haunt me

with that longing to venture out again,
to explore the high streams, the salt wave's play,
to discover once more in my travels
strange peoples in unknown lands.

Yet throughout the earth's expanse
there is not one single sailor
so proud of spirit or hearty in youth,
so gracious in giving or noble in deeds,

none so beloved of his lord
that he has not a secret fear
as to what his voyage may hold,
what Wyrd may do to him.

But for the mariner nothing else suffices—
not the harp's sound nor prize of gilded rings,
not his wife's caress nor world's bliss,
naught but the rolling of waves.

An aging seafarer always feels this hunger
when the groves bloom and villages become fair,
when the plains grow green and the whole earth stirs,
urges his eager heart to sail out again.

So it is for me, old as I am in years,
that the voice of the cuckoo, warm summer's herald,
sings a mournful note, becomes a harbinger
of bitter cares in my breast-hoard.

The retainer, that happy warrior round the hearth,
can never know what I have known,
I who pace the wide and solitary paths,
how my deepest heart yearns now in its cage.

My grey spirit yet aches for the sea-flood,
and my mind's thought fares out far and wide
over the whale's home and the vast expanse of earth,
then returns greedy, eager for more.

The lone-flier yells to me, taunts me relentlessly,
to sail out on the whale's path, the sea's breadth—
desires hotter around my heart than all earth's joy,
than all the dying life so fleeting on the shore.

For well I know earthly treasure never lasts;
each man awaits one of three things;
illness, age, or the Slayer's sword.
The fated one must ever go deprived of life.

For every atheling—even the mightiest of earls—
there remains at the end of this life
only the praise earned from living men
recited after death.

THE SCOP'S PLAINT
ca. 8th century AD

Weland became an exile because of the sword.
That sturdy earl suffered hardship,
had for companions torment and longing,
often knew misery in winter—cold exile
after Nith had bound him in fetters.
Slender sinews constrained the better man.
> That passed.
> So may this.

To Beadohild her brother's death
was not so grievous as her own care
when she discovered she was with child.
Never might she think contentedly
how that could be resolved.
> That passed.
> So may this.

I have heard about Maethhild,
how for her the Geat's love became so boundless
that it bereaved him of sleep.
> That passed.
> So may this.

For thirty winters Theodoric
ruled the Maering's dwelling.
That is known to many.
> That passed.
> So may this.

We have heard of Eormanric's wolflike thoughts;
widely he ruled the kingdom of the Goths.
That was a grim king.
Many a man sat bridled by grief
awaiting more woe and often wishing
that the kingdom would be overthrown.
> That passed.
> So may this.

One in misery sits bereft of joy,
thinks to himself with brooding spirit
that his share of sorrow is endless.
Then may he ponder how throughout the world
the wise Lord directs the affairs of men.
For many an earl He decrees honor and fame,
and for some a portion of hardship.

I will say this about myself
that for a while I was the Heodeninga's scop,
so precious to my lord that Deor was my name.
For many winters I had a good post, a gracious lord,
until now, Heorrenda, a song-crafty man,
has received the land-right
that the protector of earls once gave me.
                    That passed away.
                    So may this.

from WIDSITH
'The Far Wandering One'
ca. 7th century AD

To keep a drowsy Emperor awake;
Or set upon a golden bough to sing
To lords and ladies of Byzantium
Of what is past, or passing, or to come.
                              W.B. Yeats

The far wandering scop spoke
unlocked his word-hoard,
he who more than other men,
had known all the races and nations
throughout the earth,
who had received burnished gold
as reward in the hall.

His forebears sprang from the Myrgings.
He was with Ealhhild,
the gracious peace-weaver;
from the Angels in the east
he first sought the home of Eormanric,
the savage faithless Gothic king.
He began then to speak many things:

'Because I have known so many
rulers throughout the earth,
I have come to understand
how a prince must live justly
if he wishes his throne to prosper,
one earl to succeed another.

I have travelled this wide world
to many foreign lands.
Both good and evil have I suffered,
parted from my kinsmen,
far from my own hearth companions.
Wherefore might I recite in the halls
how noble princes were generous to me.

I was with the Huns and the glorious Goths,
with the Swedes and with Geats,
with the Angles and the Vikings,
with the Saxons and the Danes.
With the Franks was I, and the Frisians,
with the Glommas and the Romans.

I was with the Greeks and Finns
with Caesar who held sway over bright cities,
who had riches and the Welsh kingdom.
I was with the Scots and Picts,
with the Israelites and Assyrians,
I was with the Medes and Persians,
with the Myrgings and Mofdings.

And princes, mighty kings I knew.
Their names I can recite even now:

Hwala was for a time the best
and Alexander the mightiest of all;
Aetla ruled the Huns,
Eormanric the Goths,
Becca the Banings,
Gifca the Burgundians.
Caesar ruled the Greeks
and Caelic the Finns,
Theodric ruled the Franks,
Gefwulf the Jutes,
Offa ruled the Angles,
Alewih the Danes.

Thus we scops go wandering among men
to many lands as fate decrees;
we seek a dwelling, a prince,
one wise in heart and liberal in gifts
who desires to exalt his fame,
to preserve his valorous deeds among men.
For after light and life fall in ruin,
the scop may fashion praise into poems
and chant the warrior's lofty glory
far and wide among nations under the skies.'

THE EXILE
ca. early 8th century AD

I

The solitary one often prays for grace
as he wanders wearily over the water
sometimes rowing with his bare hands
in the frost-cold sea—Wyrd is relentless.

Thus alone I must at each day's dawning
recount aloud my wretched plight
since now there is none alive to whom
I might open plainly the door to my heart.

Yes, I know it is a noble custom
for a warrior to bind fast his breast-care,
safeguard his hoard-coffer
whatever he might feel

for a weary mind can do naught against Wyrd
nor do words from an angry heart bring solace,
so those who seek glory conceal their pain
in the recesses of their soul.

And thus I, bereft of homeland, of kinsmen,
reeking of grief, have sealed with fetters
my own heart's wound now that the dark earth
has eaten my good gold-friend.

2

Abject and wild with winter's woe,
I come thence over frozen waves
to seek the hall of a good treasure-giver
who might understand my need.

He who has felt such solitude
knows how cruel a comrade is sorrow
for one bereft of the company of friends.
No wound gold for him, no fruit of the fields,

only a freezing corpse and dark thoughts—
images of warriors strutting in the hall,
the doling of treasures at the feast,
how his gold-friend indulged him in youth.

All that is vanished with the wise counsel of elders;
anguish and sleep coalesce in dreams;
he thinks he clasps his liege-lord,
on the king's knee lays his weary head.

Then he awakens and sees before him
fallow waves on the sea-bird's bath,
falling snow mixed with hail,
and his heart's wound is more grievous still.

Thoughts of his kinsmen course through his mind;
he thinks he greets them with gladness,
gazes eagerly at spectral visions,
but the spirits sing no familiar songs.

3

When one wise in thought, sage in spirit,
carefully considers the ruined walls,
the slaughter of kinsmen and this somber life,
he chants to himself this old refrain:

Where has the horse gone?
Where has the kinsman gone?
Where has the treasure-giver gone?
Where is the mead hall?

Where are all the joys of feast?
O the bright cup!
O the warrior striding in his mail-shirt!
O the majesty of the prince!

How that time has passed away,
become hidden under night's helm
as if it never existed;
only crumbling walls remain.

The might of the ash-spear has taken the earls,
slaughter-greedy weapons and Wyrd the mighty one.
Winter's terror now binds the earth
when shadows come, send from the north

harsh hailstorms as mischief to men,
for all is wretched in earth's kingdom;
Wyrd's ingenuity knows how to disorder
this world beneath the sky.

Here possessions are fleeting.
Here friends are fleeting.
Here woman is fleeting.
All this earthly place becomes idle, desolate.

THE RUIN
ca. 8th century AD

Whither are gone the proud and their palaces? Gaze thou into their tombs, that thou mayest profit by this example, inasmuch as We made it a lesson unto every beholder.

Bahá'u'lláh, Tablet to Napoleon III

Wondrous stone wall   cracked by Wyrd;
village dwellings   burst apart,
the work of giants   crumbled.
Roofs are sunken   towers brought down,
ornate barred gate   despoiled.
Frost is on the mortar,   the shingles sheared;
all is eaten   by the ages.
Earth's grasp   has long since seized
the crafty men,   a hundred generations
come and gone;   only this wall endures
grey with lichen,   stained red,
weathering storms   kingdom after kingdom.

THE WITAN CONSULTS
ON STOICISM
8th century AD

Should prosperity befall thee, rejoice not, and should abasement come upon thee, grieve not, for both shall pass away and be no more.

Bahá'u'lláh

Speak to me in plain words,
let not thy thoughts be hidden,
thy inmost wisdom withheld—

I will not reveal my secrets
if you keep from me your mind's craft.
Sage ones should share their insight.

First let us praise God well
since He loaned us this life and brief joy;
and he will remind us of these gifts.

Man's dwelling is on earth
where the young must grow old,
for only God is eternal.

Fates cannot change Him
nor can aught harm the Almighty,
neither time nor disease.

He grows not old in spirit
but yet remains as he ever was,
a patient prince.

He gives us our own thoughts,
varied minds, many voices,
because the kin of men inhabit

many islands the Creator formed
for the diverse customs
and different tribes.

And so people must consult,
wise ones with the wise,
until their minds are in accord.

Only this can settle strife,
restore the peace that vile ones
have taken away from us.

Such counsel is apt for sage ones,
as is justice for the just,
and goodness for the good.

People are bound together:
a man and woman beget children,
bring them into the world through pain.

But every tree on earth
must in time lose its leaves,
lament its lost branches;

all the fated ones must go,
every doomed one die,
though daily he bewail this separation.

The Creator of this middle dwelling
alone knows when that death shall come,
who shall leave his homeland.

He brings forth infants
which early illness takes,
but if He did not lessen our numbers

there would be too many over the earth
among the race of men,
no limit to kin-timber.

Thus foolish is he who knows not God,
for death comes unexpected.
Wise ones protect their souls,

keep their covenant righteously.
Happy is he who thrives on earth
and wretched if friends desert him.

He shall not be glad
whose sufficiency fails him,
for he shall be bound by need,

but blessed ever are the baleless ones,
while the blind shall curse their eyes
when clear vision is withheld from them;

No more do they behold the stars,
nor the bright sun nor the moon,
and that will harrow their hearts,

but if they conceal pain inside,
how can they expect
that change will ever come?

PART THREE

Great Grandfather's Curious Letters

Mine eyes have seen the glory of the coming of the Lord;
He is trampling out the vintage where the grapes of wrath
    are stored
He hath loosed the fateful lightning of His terrible swift
    sword:
    His truth is marching on.
                    Julia Ward Howe

ONE FOR MARY JANE

Hampshire, Tennessee
May 29, 1854

read yours of the 17th
(at the proper time)
and was quite gratified
to have the pleasure
of once more reading
an Epistle from your fair hand.

Such letters as your last, Mary,
have a reviving influence
that acts upon my mind

like the refreshing dew drops
upon the wilted flowers
that give to them new life
and raise their drooping heads,

like the invigorating May showers
that cause the tender buds
to issue forth in their fragrance
and beauty.

Mary, I truly thank you
for the sweet poem
and will ever cherish it
as from the nearest and dearest
friend to my heart on earth,
and consider it so far superior
to anything of the kind I have seen
I cannot presume to answer it
in the form of
a poem.

Spottswood Henry Hatcher

GREAT GRANDFATHER'S
CURIOUS LETTERS

Fighting backward toward Atlanta, he
watched his Franklin, Tennessee, farm
descend one of the foothill knolls
that rose before him like green blisters

the fading of the fence-fitted world.
Later the paper scraps would come home,
dragged by a disfigured or war-rattled
neighbor. The lettered lines would

swirl and crowd the parchment leaf,
finally pushed from the page at a chewed-
off edge; only the letter-loop spaces
showed the nondescript yellow-grey-brown.

Yet these were lessons in dignity: the
cataloguing of the dead (Franklin boys,
town square shouts short months before);
the prospect scanned (Kennesaw behind

him, the small farm houses like his own
dotting the red clay hills); the passion-
less plea for order (care for the coloreds,
a Christian moulding for the children).

He fought backward toward Atlanta as
if raised for nothing else, almost
easily—as he would swing a scythe on
a cool evening when the hay, moist and

heavy, was felled naturally and nobly like
well stroked pines. He had no reason to
be there; the troops that trampled his
green corn were his own, taking a back

path to the Columbia pike. Still, he
fought backward with his English musket,
tin spoon, and mess kit as though this
were some annual spring rite. Perhaps

the soil roots taught him to expect
disorder, or at best the seasons;
and he fought as he would tend his
crop after hail—pursuing what seemed

to him the natural course of things.
But that November morning as he heard
behind him in the distance the popping
muskets and vibrating bass of cannon,

the Christian and father and farmer
in him gauged with awful certitude
the lack of similarity between a smooth
rifle stock and a worn wood scythe handle.

SIGNS OF SPRING

*The arrival of Bahá'u'lláh in the Najíbíyyih Garden [in April, 1863] . . .
signalizes the commencement of what has come to be recognized as the holiest and
most significant of all Bahá'í festivals.*

Shoghi Effendi

Tullahoma, Tennessee
April 11, 1863

The doctor says I have the jaundice
and we hear rumors that the Yankees
are leaving Murfreesboro and falling back
to Nashville or perhaps into Kentucky—

I would be very glad if we
could move safely towards Nashville

*so few miles between us
except for the enemy lines
and burning fields
and our country burning*

I hope they may never come to see you.
I suppose they have committed
many depredations in Williamson County,
burning College Grove,
even the churches—
I don't see how such conduct can prosper

unless God be ruled by wicked men
and the course of things not set firm
after all the prayers and days
of tending after crops and the stock,
trying, always trying to do
the right thing.

If God lets this war continue
until wickedness ceases in the army,
you might safely say it has just begun
unless He changes the hearts of soldiers
very materially,
for it looks to me like
they certainly get no better.

But I hope & pray
the days of peace & joy
may soon dawn on upon us again.

Of course, it is worse with me out here
than it is with you at home—
not one of my dear sweet little family
to cheer my lonely hours
and you with the company of our children
to divert your mind.

Mary, God only knows
when we shall meet again.
I expect to pass through many trials;
I am trying to live as near right as I can
and if it is God's will
that I shall never return home,
I hope to meet you where
war's dearth and sorrow
are never known.

I have strong hope of getting home—
I believe I will be spared to live
with you and the children again—

(if I had about a gallon
of your good apple vinegar,
I could soon cure the jaundice.)

I long to hear from home sweet home
where time has passed so pleasantly & happily
and where I hope to spend with you
and with our dear little ones
many a happy day when this scourge
shall have passed from our land,
when God shall have driven away
the clouds that hang so heavy over our heads
that threaten us with temporal destruction
already laying waste our nation
and taking the lives of our dear countrymen.

But thanks be to God
they cannot kill the soul
and He has told us to fear
not man but rather him who could kill
both soul and body.

They may kill my body
and part me from my dear loved ones
for a season,
but I have a hope of life
beyond this vale of tears,

where we will outlive
all sorrow and gloom
where no dark clouds hang over us
where wars shall not disturb
our peaceful mirth,
where all shall be
peace, joy, and love.

I hope to see you
and my dear little children
in that blessed land
where the weary are at rest
and the wicked cease from troubling.

My daily prayer is that we
may soon be reunited in peace
and finally reunited
a family unbroken in Heaven.

TELL ME ABOUT YOUR GARDEN

Japonica
Glistens like coral in all of the neighbouring gardens,
And today we have naming of parts
Henry Reed

Tullahoma, Tennessee
April 21, 1863

tell me about your garden,
the stock, the colts,
the lambs, and hogs,
the clover, wheat

(especially the children)—

don't let the cattle
on the clover too soon;
they will eat it so close
it will not do much good.

Give my respects
to all our family—
both black and white—
and kiss our little children for me.

I can not censure you
for taking the oath,
for I know not under what circumstances
you took it;

it was rather mortifying to my feelings
when I first learned it,
but shall not complain
at anything you do—

I have confidence and believe
that you will always do
what you think best
under all conditions.

Just go ahead
and do as you wish
with all our concerns
and I shall be quiet.

(don't you think that nice talk
to be telling you to do as you please
when I am way off here
where I can't help myself?)

I want you all
to pray for me and for peace
and for our many friends and loved ones
that are in the army.

Give my respects to all the family,
kiss the children and tell them
something nice from me—
that Pa loves them a great deal.

Forgive the bad writing
and everything in my letter
that you think
I should not have written.

Good bye, dear wife.

A CIVIL WAR

Hearken ye, O Rulers of America and the Presidents of the Republics therein,
unto that which the Dove is warbling on the Branch of Eternity.

Bahá'u'lláh

camp near Dalton, Georgia
March 20, 1864

My Dear Wife and Children,
I know you must be very anxious
to hear from me.
I start a letter
every two or three weeks
but I don't know
whether you receive them or not.
I have not received a letter from you
since some time in December, 1863.

The question often presents itself to my mind—
shall I ever be permitted to return in peace
to my dear little family
and my beloved parents and friends again.

because I have known
the names that strike terror in our hearts—
Missionary Ridge, Chickamauga Creek—
I can tell of eyes that stare out in wonder
comrades draped across the boulders

rock won't you hide me on that day?

I have felt the shells crashing
through brilliant autumn leaves
like intruders from some lethal planet
and old Charlie Davis caught by surprise
somewhere between his amazing leap
over the fallen tree and landing
limp in the trench beside me
wordless

Often I think of how I would be received
if I could be permitted to return home
and picture to my mind
how you and the children look.
They have grown so much since I saw them
and perhaps changed in appearance

*Charlie left his feet grinning
gasping something like 'Boy!' or 'Whee!'
and became so changed I did not know him*

I dreamed of nursing Mary last night.
I thought she was walking & talking.
She seemed to know me.
It surprised me that she was not
afraid of me;
She hugged and kissed me.

*we leave a trail of lives behind us;
we are pursued two to one
retreating from what? Tyranny?
My own sovereign government?
And which is sovereign after all?*

We have a revival of religion here

*sensing we cannot forever outlast,
out-maneuver Sherman's every
shrewd plan to outflank us,
and Johnson's masterful retreat
not aggressive enough for the high command,
who would not turn to faith?*

There have been several conversions
—I don't know how many.
I would be so much delighted
to attend church at old Thomases again
and hope that I may be permitted to do so
when this war shall have passed away
& peace once more restored to our country

and peace restored to every land
and the spring promise
more than longer marches
and rain and mud
and me in my orderly garden
and the corn bread and fresh beans
and dripping sweet tomatoes
on our good white china plates
so deserved after all day
in the broiling country sun.

COUNTING THE DEAD
(a few days before the battle of Atlanta)

July 8, 1864
camp on the Chattahoochee River

Mary,
there is no use in trying to describe
what we have passed through since May 10th,
under arms nearly all the time
and always in hearing of balls and shells.
Abe and I have both come out unhurt so far
and I earnestly pray that God in much mercy
may continue to spare us.

Our company has been quite unlucky—
we have lost three killed dead
and Capt. Wilson now seriously
if not mortally wounded—
I fear he will not recover.

The killed in our company are:
F.C. Russel,
E.A. Williams
and O.C. Wilson.

John Waddy was wounded on the 15th of May
and it is thought that he is dead.
George Greeman has been killed.
Jordan of the 20th was wounded and is dead.
Bob Fleming has lost his leg.
W. Price has lost his left arm
(I think it was his left).
George McConnico was wounded in the hand.

We have been falling back slowly
and attended with some loss of men,
but I believe we have the advantage
most of the time.
In several engagements
we know the enemy has suffered severely.
It is remarkable how the men endure hardships
and what spirits they continue in—

of course,
we all very much dread being shot
and there are some good men
falling around us every day,
but nearly all think the war
is drawing to a close,
or at least that this
will be the last year
(God grant that it may be).

Mary,
I am staying here trying to do my duty
not because I do not dread fighting
or that I wilfully stay away from you
and my sweet little children,
nor can I tell you I would pass through again
what we have experienced in the last two months
for all the wealth of the world—
yet there may be just as bad in store for us
and doubtless many of us will yet
fall victim to this cruel war.

Mary,
I greatly desire to be spared
to return to my family in peace
(it may be my desire is too great).

I want to live and die in peace
at home with my loved ones around me.

I want to be spared to try to lead my children
to the rock that is higher than I

to instruct them and influence them
to yield submissively to the will of God

and to obey his commandments.

I think sometimes
that I am not really afraid of death,
but I very much dread death at the hands of men—
I prefer falling into the hands of my Maker
and I thank and praise His name
that He has spared me thus far.

Mary,
don't distress yourself about me
but turn your attention to your children
and if I should never be permitted
to return to you again,
try to raise them right
and instill the right principles within.

Mary,
don't think because I warn you about the children
in almost every letter
that I have not full confidence in you
as a Christian and as a faithful parent
for I believe you will try to do your duty.

But there is so much wickedness
and careless negligence in the land
and so many dying without hope in Christ
that I want it deeply and forcibly
and lastingly impressed upon their minds,
the necessity of a Godly life
of trusting in the atoning merits
of the blood of Christ,
of making it their aim in life
to give God the praise
and at last to obtain
an admittance into Heaven.

Impress upon their minds
that worldly honor and possessions
are not lasting
and not so much to be desired.

Give my love and respect to all my friends
and especially to my parents
and to you, my sweet little children,
and to Mira, Julian and their children,
and if we never meet on earth again,
God grant that we may meet in that better land
where all is joy and peace.

Your husband,

Spottswood Henry Hatcher

THE BATTLE OF ATLANTA

it is an ever fixed mark
That looks on tempests and is never shaken
                              Shakespeare

near Love Joy Station, Georgia
September 9, 1864
(8 days after the Battle of Atlanta)

Dear Wife & Children
I am thankful
that God has still
been merciful to me
and permitted me
to write to you

that my life is still spared
after many bloody scenes,
that He has brought me safely
through all the conflicts
that we have just endured:

June 27th, Kennesaw Mountain, 4600
dead, wounded or missing—Federal victory

July 20, Peachtree Creek, 4796
dead, wounded or missing—Federal victory

July 28, Ezra Church, 4642
dead, wounded or missing—Federal victory

August 31–September 2, Atlanta, 2000
dead wounded or missing—Federal victory

I hope I may be spared to return
to my loved ones again
and I pray God to speed the day
when I may enjoy such happiness.

Days are passing swiftly,
though it seems like a long time
since I saw you
and my sweet little children

Mary, I have seen villages
burned to the ground
farm houses like our own
splinter before the cannonade,
have heard, actually heard
minie balls hiss by my ear,
so close was I to leaving you.
I have seen men plucked
randomly from infantry lines
from trees and trenches—
a beardless boy from Murphresboro
who moments before had sworn to me
he was no longer afraid

Yes, it is long when I am separated
from those that are ever nearest my heart,
those whom I love more dearly
than all others besides.

But I am still alive
still husband and father
still believe in the ordered life
and the duty implanted in my soul

Tell the boys to be good boys
to obey Ma and not to learn bad words,
and if they are disposed to use bad words,
tell them that Pa don't do that way,
that Pa never swore in his life,
that they never heard
Gran Pa or Uncle John swear,
that good boys don't swear.

O, Dear Mary,
I try to imagine
how you and the children look
and how each one would do
could we be so blessed as to meet.
What a pleasure indeed it would be
could peace be restored
and we return to our families again.

SHERMAN'S MARCH TO THE SEA

outside Atlanta, Georgia
September 23, 1864

We have been resting longer since the 3rd of this month
without being under fire than at any time
since the first week in May.

I can't write you any war news that is of any
account to you, for you can see more in the paper
than I can write.

I often dream of being with you and the children
—I don't know how many times last night
I did dream of being with loved ones.

I would awake to find it only a dream
and doze off again
and be nursing and playing with the children.

Henry was so fond of me
that he could not stay away
and I would pet him and tell him he was Pap's boy.

At one time I thought I had Mary in my arms
and was giving her something to eat or drink.
At first she seemed contented with me.

All at once she discovered
that she was not acquainted with me
and she would not stay.

DESERTION

My friend, you would not tell with such high zest
To children ardent for some desperate glory,
The old Lie: 'Dulce et decorum est
Pro patria mori.'

Wilfred Owen

outside Atlanta, Georgia
September 27, 1864

It's true as you say
some leave the army and return to Tennessee.
Yes, many of them have deserted,

but you must know that I would never desert,
but I can say to you I would not go any man's surety
for there is no telling who will give way to temptation—

This is certainly a place to try men's souls,
but I have thought how sad you would be
and what a weight would be upon my own mind

were I to desert and come home:
my presence would annoy you
for you would feel that I had disgraced myself

and placed a stigma upon my children
that would follow us to our graves,
though the time may come when I shall conclude

that it would be best for me to come to my family—
We know not what changes may take place,
and while I feel it my duty

to be subject to the powers that be, to serve my country,
I also feel it a duty binding upon me to take care of
the little family that God has seen fit to give me.

I have turned it over in my mind again and again.
It seems I could not make as useful a man
after this war shall have ended

were I to desert as if I had remained
true to the oath I have taken.
I have a great desire to return and raise my children

to worship again around the family altar
to live and instruct my children
that we may lead them to Christ

that we may so reflect the light of Christ
that others may be influenced
to come to that light which shineth away all darkness.

CHOOSING:
THE BATTLE OF FRANKLIN
November 30, 1864

Thy firmness makes my circle just,
And makes me end where I begun.
John Donne

It was not shirking his duty to pursue the higher good.
It was not walking over familiar roads and fields
and not exactly the smell of hickory fires
banked in the small frame farmhouses
and not exactly sensing how really close he was to home—
life was always a matter of choosing.

Marching, marching again
now full circle hurrying up through Alabama
just in time to salvage the wooden pride
of the pure bred West Point grad,
Great Grandfather had not wanted to return like this,

to see his own town a sordid arena for this wickedness,
to see the familiar landscapes charred after the harvest—
not at all the homecoming of his late night reverie.

And when that evening at Spring Hill the officers
toasted their advantage with real Tennessee sippin' whiskey—
having arrived early, the Federals fast on their heels—
Great Grandfather waited with the other footsoldiers
entrenched in the gentle slopes
on either side of the Columbia pike
unconcerned that the fighting general
might at long last reclaim his good name.

Great Grandfather watched their carousing light
then looked the few miles eastward toward home,
smiled as he remembered that this was his birthday—
thirty-four years old and no one at all to tell
how God had indeed returned him alive and well.
Yet even so ironic a conceit
could not coax his dutiful mind.

He reviewed the expressionless men—
all men now, even the very young
who had no children waiting,
whose microcosm had become but the numbing march
and the fitful dreamfilled sleep,
the nightmare cannon,
the gunsmoke fog and rancid sweet smell
of neglected flesh and smouldering flesh
and twisted rag dolls of bodies
dropped from the late November sky
like spindled colorless leaves.

And when he awoke in the night to the scuffling feet
of weary Union troops and rumbling Federal caissons,
he waited like a vulture perched on a dying tree,
his long and heavy musket cold against his stubbled cheek,
and saw down his sights another farmer growing old,
a footsoldier marching, doing as he was told.

Great Grandfather watched his own bewildered comrades
who shook their shadowed heads in silent knowing,
acquiescing to the non-command,
and instantly he knew that all the wars he waged
had suddenly come to an end.

By late morning as the lieutenants strapped
Hood's one remaining leg to a noble mount,
and he lifted his one remaining arm
to signal advance against the same army
he had in the night drunkenly allowed
to slip between them like water.

He did not see and could not have understood
the rancor in the faces of his men
but by noon as he tried to rally them
through fatal trenches up against the Federal wall
there was nothing left in their eyes
but a bitter resolve not ever to fight again,
not for worn-out causes or someone's sad career.
They fought to live out one more day
that somehow like Great Grandfather they
might find their way back home again.

Waiting for the Messiah

And now with gleams of half-extinguished thought,
With many recognitions dim and faint,
And somewhat of a sad perplexity,
The picture of the mind revives again . . .
William Wordsworth

STARMOUNT FOREST PROLOGUE

> *. . . I sang in my chains like the sea*
> Dylan Thomas

I knew the world globed
but like the Hebrew children before me,
thought we were on the inside,
the heavens a crystalline blue sphere
and the earth settled on the bottom
so that beyond the horizon of
Starmount Forest was a fine line
where meadow met shell of sky
and I wanted to touch it,
to run my finger tips along the seam,
to trace the boundaries of my life.

LA BELLE DAME EXPLAINS THE INJUSTICES OF COLONIALISM AND THE FIRST LAW OF THERMODYNAMICS

. . . we were admitted to the sight of apparitions . . . which we behold shining in pure light, pure ourselves and not yet enshrined in that living tomb which we carry about, now that we are imprisoned in the body, like an oyster in his shell.

Socrates

Some nights in the midst of a sleep
more real than houses
a blond maiden in blue silk gown
would lead me into the dense forest
behind Nonnie Burwell's house
where vines covered bushes and dogwood
making secret chambers in the snow
I never showed to anyone.

There she comforted me, nurtured me,
knew me perfectly and has never left,
has mercy, pity, wisdom,
and never allows me to despair.
She vindicates the world of children,
verifies the joy and justice
they suspect infused into
the very fabric of the universe.

It was she who informed me
as I watched cars accelerate
up the hill in front of our house
that nothing really works like that—
the mere push of a pedal.
As with my bicycle,
somehow, somewhere, someone
always must pay.

THIMBLE THIMBLE

in a circle of prayer
we sit,
hands in place,
palm on palm,
waiting wordless
for the slicing between
thumbs and fingers,
the parting of seas,
the tickling skin;

will it drop
or will it
not?
will a
snicker
show it?

no matter,
it is
the slithering hands
between hands
so cool and intimate
we wait for.

THE PASSING TRAIN

Because I was a child before
the passenger train became
immoral
I count among
my favorite relics

proud coaches—
polished brass handrails
and starched white
antimacassars;

I knew porters
by their names,
what the whistles said,
what the dots and dashes meant
on trackside signs;

at small-town stops
I helped raise the door
that covered the steps,
felt the magic in dragon breath
that hissed from the belly
of the train
smelling like rain
on a summerhot street;

inside I ran the aisles
to fetch water
in foldable cups
while farms blurred by
wheat-colored;

I sought out
secret principalities:

the men's room
draped like a stage
stainless steel
and ivory buttons
to squirt soap;
the john flushed
with a pedal push,

the sun reflecting
off the crossties
right through
the belly of the train!

the purgatorial chamber
between the cars,
a roaring room
where clanking metal sang
like a funhouse circus
machine;
so hard to push
that wind-sucked door,
hard to stand
without holding on
but when alone
I practiced,
or through the opened
top half-door
poked my head
to feel the wind
or around a bend
see every car
from the engine back.

At mealtime
I entered the dining car
unsure—
it was carnations and
white linen,
disdainful of
questions,
though once I ordered
kadota figs for breakfast
and they tasted of nectar
like their name;
I watched
restless cars
stopped at crossings
waiting for us to pass
so envious
of our fine restaurant.

After the afternoon
games of chase
through corridors
and passageways,
the inevitable crash
into an old lady's frown
someone changed
our coach seat
into a sleeping room
complete
with ironed sheets,
a net for shoes,
a special light,
an adjustable vent—
all this happened
while I was
somewhere else.

Then bedtime rites
and everyone finally asleep
but me,
I inched up the green shade,
cast omniscient eyes

on weary truckers
plugging along
country roads
thinking themselves
alone,

on rows of streetlights
guarding
silent, patterned
villages,

but before too long
the cradle rocking
the track clacking
could close my eyes
no matter how hard
I always tried
to make it stay
forever.

TETHERED CHILD

For mothers are the first educators, the first mentors; and truly it is the mothers who determine the happiness, the future greatness, the courteous ways and learning and judgment, the understanding and the faith of their little ones.

'Abdu'l-Bahá

mother, you are out there
at the end of my rope

holding me down
axiomatically;

I sit at night
deskside, penpoised

waiting for a muse
to goose me

waiting for love
from a trap door;

your unguents cannot now
nor chicken soup suffice me;

cordbound, clayshod
crude borne in the dark,

I await your messages,
all the pretty names

the panaceac creams
as the slack is taken up

and the kitechild drifts
to his limits.

HAMILTON LAKE
Greensboro, North Carolina (1946)

After a time he enters the period of youth in which his former conditions and needs are superseded by new requirements applicable to the advance in his degree.

'Abdu'l-Bahá

Always it was too cold in the spring,
but no sooner had the calendar spoken
and the iris bulbs my mother guarded with her life
exploded obscenely into purple
with honey yellow centers,
than we piled high and squealing
into the back seat of the real wood station wagon
and headed for Hamilton Lake.

The name itself had the taste of water,
and as we passed the last rows of houses,
rambled out the winding rural road,
trees thickened into leafy green walls
so that every curve looked alike
and neither brother nor I could guess
how far, how long, or if in the course of winter
some demon had stolen the lake away.

Then to see the first silver shot of sunlight
reflecting through the base of trees,
and always after the one turn
I had given up on;
a left down the dirt road
as images jerked through the limbs
like flashing light on the silent screen:
fishermen waiting in wooden rowboats;
slender boys poised at the top
of the tall white diving tower
from which only the bravest would jump
into the dark waters below.

At last to stand on the concrete dock
whose warmed surface felt rough
on my winter tender feet;
the clean cool breeze bristled my cotton hair
and we stood watching the water, the tower,
waiting for a courage sufficient
to move us out through the spring air
over the spring-fed waters
exchanging the comforting sun
for the chest-jolting cold
of that first leap of faith.

We watched each other endlessly
(never asking why it must be this way)
until the compulsion of need
could no longer be denied—
the legs worked by themselves
jumping the body out into inescapable space,
the nerves just waiting to tell the brain
exactly how unnatural this really was—

the body suddenly paralyzed with a nettled chill,
the toes skittering along the murky bottom;
the automatic arms propelling us
towards escape up the ladder rungs,
through even colder air
into a towel cocoon stretched out ready,
a father's hand at either end,
a knowing smile in the middle.

Never again! Never again!

Until the sun smoothed down the goose flesh
and the matted hair once more fluttered
and all the pain was forgiven and forgotten
by the fathomless mercy of children
whose laws defy all stasis
and who in time forsake even
a father's warm embraces.

FLYING DREAMS

summer dusk
still light out
but eight o'clock
did not care;
authentic white fur
of the stuffed rabbit
against my cheek,
affectionate pink marble eyes
watching with me the wind
work the pines outside my window.

Soon I was off
in search of flight.
a power that was in me
whether in crowds or alone—
not to flap exactly,
not to need to,
but to run, run until
the expanse of my arms
was sufficient for currents
to ease me up

only inches at first,
then clearing treetops,
turning and swooping
over the neighbors
who watched in awe.

Instinctively I knew
how pride could bring me down
because I was never really
in control, never foreknowing
exactly when if ever
I might fly again

but often
at the edge of sleep
I prayed for just
one more flying dream
to inform me what there was
worth striving for.

WAITING FOR THE MESSIAH

Truly I say to you, whosoever does not receive the kingdom of God like a child shall not enter it.

Christ

Later I learned that early lights
were an insult to baby Jesus

(a week after Thanksgiving was quite soon enough)
but the whole year wheeled around that day

and the hours between me and the magic of that morning
stood like stone sentinels I had to slay one at a time.

My passion swelled as the macrocosm teased my senses
portending advent of more than sled or skates.

The radio at last began to carol,
as mother gently unpacked the hand-carved crèche

with its delicate camels, real hay, and holy infant
so tiny I could have swallowed him.

Then at last was the huge faded red box
packed to the brim with shining balls,

tinsel, and beads, strings of stars,
angel hair, elves, icicles, birds, and French horns,

each with a past and piece that was missing
but placed at last on our pagan tree.

The whole town arrayed itself
in evergreen and gaudy strands of light;

bells rang out while passersby filled pots with coin;
confirmed my faith in the universal law of *Magic*!

Eternally fixed and firm as gravity,
natural as seasons, no child's fairy myth

but a general accord that heavenly justice
would reign supreme in the bleakest streets,

overwhelm the hardest hearts, infest even
the implacable ritual of father's workaday world.

And when the night of the Promised One finally came,
ushered in by hymns and festive candles,

sleep came only from the sheer will
of wanting that last night to dwindle

into the dusky morning of affirmation
when in the faint light of a barely risen sun,

brother and I would tumble down stairs
to see once more the splendid radiance,

the symmetrical display of celestial plenitude
made utterly corporeal by an iconic elf.

And when I asked Dad where the bottle cap was
from the soda we left out annually for an enervated god,

it was not from faltering conviction, as he supposed,
but to know more perfectly the ways of God to man.

And the laws of retribution they had taunted me with—
sticks and coal for the recalcitrant—

no idle threats, but dreaded possibility
to one who harbored a trove of secret sin.

So on the morning of Christ's nativity
when I saw no briary twigs in the stocking,

I knew firsthand the abundance of holy grace,
and the span of God's omniscience;

He had known, after all, what parents never could:
—the difference between a tin wind-up train

with its unnatural key sticking out of the side
and the finely tooled black steel of a Lionel engine.

SNAPSHOT!
FIRST DAY OF SCHOOL
September, 1946

On the starting line I wait,
sweaty hands by my side,
outfit large enough for growing into
and stiffly new, smelling of new.

What's it going to be, little tableau,
this institute they're taking you to?
Why all the trussing up, cameras out,
the motor running, summer really gone?

Why is your mother smiling so oddly?
And why the manilla folder
you may carry but are forbidden to open
because it contains 'supplies'?

Child of my dreams,
if only I could sit you down
and explain how you are not dumb,
just five instead of six.

Your little hands that will in time
learn how to curve letters
on the lines of rough and unforgiving paper
just aren't quite ready yet;

and you fall up steps because
your feet are so much bigger
than your brain yet comprehends,
but you aren't really a *C* person,

and the pink lace girls
who will draw the perfect letters
who will not eat lumps in the flour paste
or pick their noses,

the little girls who will make *A*s
will in time not laugh
if you are patient and wait
and not get lost to crime

or the disease of indecision.
You, frozen there in fear,
poised on the brink of my life,
if only I could love you enough,

could warn you not to listen
to the voices whispering in your ears
the American mantra/hymn—
that everyone gets a second chance.

Stand in line, then.
Do not scratch or move or smile—
there's nothing funny in this;
believe me, nothing at all.

That's why your mother's face
is so strange about the eyes and mouth.
She's telling you goodbye,
she's telling you goodbye.

HOUSES

When wars raged across the seas
and polio menaced children in cities,
we escaped to my mother's old homestead
to wait out plagues and mortar fire.

I played soldier each day with a mill worker's boy
whose toy was a rifle his father brought back from Tarawa;
it had notches on the stock and a broken nib
where the bayonet was fixed.

We roamed the hedges alert to every mischief
—especially crazy Miss Alice who called out
from behind wooden shutters we could barely see
through the huge magnolia leaves.

She screamed that we would burn in hell
for killing her beautiful son.
Every night I dreamed about firefights
lying low on palm beaches or snug in jungle trees,

aiming at Crazy Alice, at Nazis, at faceless Japanese,
but always missing, always missing.
The chain of the side porch swing went up so high
I got butterflies imagining myself up there hanging on,

but with three of us pushing our feet against the columns
we could callump the back wall so hard,
the kitchen pots would crash to the floor in sequence
until a livid voice cried out, 'You Younguns!!'

The breakfast room had latticed glass doors on the cabinets
and layer upon layer of white paint and a smell
of something sweet that wasn't there anymore.
In the kitchen was a black woodburning stove.

Huge mahogany panelled doors slid out of the wall
to make the parlour private and quiet for
Uncle McNeill to pen his sermons and poems,
or trick me in a game of chess as he smoked his pipe.

His voice was smooth, confident, like a Victorian sofa.
On the floor were carpets he had brought back from China
where he and Aunt Wilda had been missionaries
before being driven out by The People's Army.

The carpets were dark red with birds, flowers,
and runes from China's dying past,
and the room reeked of an *élan vital*
from years of proper ladies and elegant men.

The staircase was lighted by an oval of stained glass—
red, yellow, blue specks—like a giant ghostly insect eye.
Cousin Tiffany caught a mouse on the landing, fed,
named him, as if she had done this all her life.

In the attic were stacks of musty books in Latin,
a faded set of the Harvard Classics,
my grandfather's medal from the New York School
of Physicians and Surgeons,

a cracked guitar whose one string
twanged a tune for the dead,
a trap door to the rooftop cupola
from where we could see the town movie theater.

The late afternoon wind rustled muslin curtains
in the bathroom while I basked in a cast iron tub;
its feet shaped like sturdy animal claws—
I was riding on the back of a hippo or a lion.

The creaking springs of the steel-framed bed
rocked me to sleep each night that summer
when a huge old wood frame house was my confidant,
unburdened itself of all its painful secrets:

Grandmother Ida's death at childbirth,
Mrs. Eugenia's bloody suicide from melancholia,
Grandfather's brief lingering after flu seared his heart
and war had slaughtered a generation's brightest hopes.

FIRST BIG SNOW

Muffled silence woke me
from the deepest sleep
to a world without cars
without birds or morning calls.

My room glowed blue
and the pine branches outside my window
were crusted and heavy;
the roof dripped with icy spears.

Breakfast?
Who could eat
when a world of sugar
was melting, melting away!

At war with thick clothes—
like nightmare villains behind me
and me unable to rise—
the galoshes would *not* fit!

The cap flaps tore at my ears,
and mother's knitted mittens
thwarted all tactility.
But at last the door was open!

The first blast of air
numbed my face,
stiffened my lips,
purified my lungs.

Carefully I worked my feet
down the slick steps
until the sure crunch
of fresh snow secured me.

Then, screaming down the hill,
violating the flawless snow,
rolling head over heels
to the bottom on my back,

I stopped, pulled up ear flaps,
slid off the mittens,
slowed down my breathing,
listened to rarified silence,

then prayed to the sun
for respite,
to leave me yet a while
in my splendid world of snow.

NECROMANCY
for Na
(Virginia Rebecca Southall Hatcher)
(1867–1951)

If I hold my breath
till I get to the corner
and step on each crack
with my left foot,
she won't die;
but death all the same
and I never followed
the black art again.

ALWAYS I HAVE WATCHED
THROUGH THESE EYES

In this album
my legs stretch
like a time-lapse flower,
my hair darkens by degrees,
my hands are holding

blocks,
a doctor's kit
a helmet,
a dog, a cat,
a basket of Easter eggs.

The skin peels off,
renews itself—
I shed it like
a reptile.
I am a birthday boy,
a cub scout
(with wolf badge
and two arrows)
I am immaculate
in a grey suit
on the way to church,
my hair slicked down
and because I
must wear a tie,
I will get a headache.

Posing, posing,
hiding my hands,
but always
I am the one
behind those eyes,
waiting for the world
to settle down out there.

I dress me in dress suits,
carry whatever
you put in my hands,
go wherever you point me,
but the eyes are always mine,
all mine.

A Rite of Passage

On this journey the traveler abideth in every land and dwelleth in every region. In every face, he seeketh the beauty of the Friend; in every country he looketh for the Beloved.

Bahá'u'lláh

HITCHHIKING THROUGH THE NORTH GEORGIA MOUNTAINS: A LAMENT FOR SIDNEY LANIER

1

Duffle bag slung over shoulder
army-surplus waterproofed smell
and the strap bites;

mountain sun beats down midday breezes
from Unicoi Gap and Tray Mountain
into Moody's Hollow and cool Soap Creek.

On either side tall green corn
crowds corners of the brief valley field
and its rich black bottom-land soil.

Alone I wait the three-mile hum
of down-shifting truck
whining down pickup.

2

Moonshine man and snaggled-tooth woman
never really stop;
flat-bed truck slows, sagging fenderless;

brown gapped teeth laugh me aboard,
and I hang on the truck back
hold hard around the hairpins

see through the cracked cab glass
snaggled-tooth woman's dirt blond hair
Silas Marner's thatched roof, colorless.

She drapes around the moonshine man
(my life in his hands at 60).
At the hilltop pause, out comes

a pint coke jug passed up;
god forbid impolity—
puff goes my breath just out of reach

exploding like inhaled fuel . . .
second-gearing once again down ribbon-tossed road,
snaggled-tooth woman smiles behind his back;

I glance away,
want no part of his red clay skin
descending Tray Mountain's backside.

3

Mister chicken inspector man
stop your dark Ford wagon for me;
turn your air-conditioning on high

tell me about all the chickens in White County
how you drive each day from Buford to Hiawassee
wearing your tie and college education

(not one degree, but two!)
five years to be a chicken inspector
and tell those rednecks what to do.

Stop your cool clean car for me
and I will listen to your lost days in town
your one sojourn into the cosmos.

4

Newt drives a two-ton
so it clings to mountain curves like a circus ride;
he spins that wheel as if unconnected,

talking all the while
about the '50 fire that singed the ridge
all the way to Jack's Gap Road

about how to lose a swarm of bees
by running through the thick bush
where only a bumble bee will follow

about how 'there ain't no blacks in all White County
nor never will be'—have a go
to Murray, North Carolina for a maid.

about the troop train coming home in WW I
and robbing the wine store in the French village—
not one bottle left behind after the water stop.

about the perverts and foreigners
taking over the country, ruining the kids,
spreading all kinds of godless things in the lowlands.

5

Out of the hills near Helen, Georgia,
down through the valleys of Hall
I saw the whole thing, Sidney;

the gurgling infant Chattahoochee
caress smooth river stones
then split the Nacoochee fields

gather force and head south to alien places;
mostly, Sidney, I met folks you never sang about
or dreamed about, or played your flute for.

WHATEVER HAPPENED TO JUNGLE JERRY?

1

One mile merges with the next.
the lush marsh turns sullen
until somewhere west of Ft. Meyers, Florida
signs begin to show us
in a sequence of faded pastels
the one, the only
Jungle Jerry!

Jungle Jerry with chimp on shoulder!

Jungle Jerry wrestling a deadly gator!

Jungle Jerry riding an ostrich!

Always my former Saturday matinee idol
is smiling in his pressed khaki shirt
politely tipping his pith helmet
beckoning us to his Jungle Paradise!

2

A tattered thatched wall hides
an oxidizing trailer.
Inside, a large fan rattles in monotone
wafting waves of animal smell
across a worn wood desk where sits
the one, the only Jungle Jerry!

feet propped,
chin on sweat-stained shirt,
two-day growth of white stubble—

Jungle Jerry snores, then moans

Jungle Jerry bobs his head

Jungle Jerry jerks back in fright!

Face weathered,
red maps of eyes
on jaundiced sclera,
a reflexed hand reaches out
a rattling voice mumbles
something about three dollars.

3

Jungle Jerry rubs his lips
rises through the mist of dreams
leads us through a back door
into the merciless tropic heat
and flaming sun of the Everglades
where stands a circle of battered cages:

one raccoon,
ears drooping
eye missing

a hairy pig,
'wild boar
detusked—
for reasons of public safety'

a snake, unmoving
'boa constrictor
stronger than . . .
fifty men!'

a battered black bear
pacing,
pacing
measuring the world

Jungle Jerry halts
tries to find words
blurred with repetition,
stares past empty cages
into the savannah bush—

the words, the words . . .
how he tamed the boar
helped Frank Buck
trap the snake barehanded
caught the grizzly without
weapon or sleight

old black bear
rocking in the sun
one foot in your pan of green water
rocking to chase the flies
rocking to ease the pain

entranced by the familiar motion
of the unenvironed psyche,
Jungle Jerry places his hands on the cage
like claws

the rocking,
the rocking,
the rocking helps a bit.

4

the signs come at us backwards now
but we know what they are showing:

Jungle Jerry young and smiling

friend to creatures of the swamp

'Guardian of the Everglades'

who will make it to Wednesday
on three dollars worth of muscatel

HEMINGWAY'S HOUSE
IN KEY WEST

More of a change than any loss of virginity.
Fear gone like an operation.
Hemingway

at 63
he matter-of-factly
slid his big toe
between the trigger
and the trigger guard
sucked the barrel tip
tasted burnt pellets
ream his tongue back
through his neck into
Rorschachs on the wall.

But the big toe
took no life—
ended the taking
to Paris, Italy,
Africa, Madrid,
Cuba and the Keys,
guiding his beloved *Pilar*
through the Florida Straits.

Now once more
he has wrought such
perfect symmetry—
no stale hoar ghost
doling out birthday interviews,
nursed like Ezra
without teeth, without pen.

The big toe only punc-
tuated Papa's art
and who are we
to question precision
in the feet of such
an artist?

CHICAGO'S NORTHWEST STATION ON THE FOURTH OF JULY

Innocent dark face,
magnificent dark eyes,
crane-hoisted monoliths,

massive tile arches
from an age of faith in
the capital dream,

this cathedral to
high finance and the truth
of Keynesianism—

our few Sunday voices
bounce from floor to wall
and back again,

get lost in the
infinite cubes of
commuterless space.

Beneath marble friezes
grey and somber from
a cinematic world

of pure black and white,
a colorless time,
I see your young dreams

already dwarfed by
these stone Americans
miming the Puritan ethic,

the errant equation
that work and plain desire
are sufficient.

Tell me, son,
is *your* life
as it should be?

Going with your gran,
are you?
Going to the park?

She sits
in stately dignity,
watches me warily,

a frank wisdom
in her cynical
yellowing eyes.

She reaches
to guard you,
her one last chance,

an inside
straight
to immortality.

Is it already
too late
for you?

In the cold neglected
elegance of this
stone incubator

that daily
spits out lives
from its terrible doors,

a solitary black man
in green uniform
rubs

domed trashcan lids
so they shine,
so they shine.

'It's nice to barbeque,'
says Gran
'Once a year it's not so bad.'

I nod and we wait out
these barren minutes
in echoed time,

try vainly to ignore
the lunatic who
staggers frenetically

among the benches,
rifles through
plastic garbage bags

pausing only
to accuse an old lady
of godless and obscene acts.

ALL I HAVE TO SHOW
AFTER CAMPING OUT FOR
TEN THOUSAND MILES AND
TAKING NOTES ON WRAPPERS

In the starladen night of the Gila Wilderness
in the mountains of New Mexico
I saw my own death creep spiderlike
and it came so close I could hear
the rumbling stomach call
across the lake and up the hillside
where once Geronimo consoled and rallied
the savaged Cherokawa.

Is it you, Goyakla, in the guise of Death
stalking while I pretend not to notice?
I see in the clear night sky
stars outnumbering, outshining,
outlasting me;
and I hear you, Goyakla,
whispering in the rustling grasses
of this haunted terrain.

Like the steady wind through the pine,
your voice tells me that once again
the children of men will leave
a narrow line in sand
along the rim of the Canyon's timeless womb
while the remnant of your tribe
squat on haunches among hidden caves
to watch and wait and learn.

CHRISTMAS EVE 1960

In the afternoon I bought a paperback
at the stalls along the Seine.
The wind was brisk but not cold,
the sky was cozily overcast,
but there was no threat of rain.

I ate dinner at a family place
where the tourists never go—
a delicate steak and *pommes frites*.

At dusk I walked the Champs Elysées,
watched a scriver chaulking the crucifixion
while tourists filled his hat.

I went to a movie called 'La Verité'—
Brigitte Bardot teasing a middle-aged man
by walking nude in his bedroom—
when I left the theater at nine,
passersby were shuffling across
the half-finished body of Christ.

After midnight mass at Notre Dame
I returned to *la place Glacier*
and my room in the small hotel
where the tourists never stay
to read about a young writer
alone in Paris on Christmas Eve.

EL METRO, 1961

In the white-tiled corridors
of the subways in Madrid
remnants of the *Guerra Civil*,
bare trunks of men,
dwell like baroque statuary
bartering their looks
for my pesetas.

LEAVING SPAIN

I left Spain gaunt and hollow-eyed
(from eating street food, the doctor said)
without a poem in my pocket
without even the address
of Maria Theresa Lopez Herrera
whom I had never had out
past ten o'clock supper time
because then her father and brothers
would know she was with an American—
and they knew what American boys did

driving their new cars on Madrid streets
while *Madrileños* huddled together on *tranvías*
or passed the evening on long walks
along the cobbled streets
with their shockingly beautiful *novias*;

only Americans got drunk on Saturday night—
Madrileños dared not lose control
and end up screaming into the lethal faces
of the well-trained Guardia Civil
the awful truth about Franco;

Americanos from the airbase
wore no uniform in town,
'Do not need to,' said Maite
as the ubiquitous women in black
hissed at a young American driver
blaring his horn on a quiet street
beneath the bridge near the *Placio Real*
where unrequited lovers regularly
leapt onto the tile roofs below.

No one cared that I was only a student,
had read *El Cantar del Mío Cid* in a language
that even they could not decipher,
could speak *Castellano sin acento*,
knew the dark secrets of the *Valle de los Caídos*
and why the rough-hewn men marched each year
the twenty-six kilometers to the statue
of ignominious victory.

I had sat on the stone seat
carved out for Filipe Segundo,
and like him had gazed out across the plains
from *El Escorial* to imagine
what worlds were left to conquer,
had watched from atop the highest parapet
of the Castle in Segovia
the fading sun paint the forests purple
while the treeless village below the cliff
was bathed in dusky bronze;

I had spent afternoons at *Corridas*
learning to distinguish between
the fumbling cruelty of the novices
and the merciful grace of a fine *rejoneador*;

On Wednesdays I lived at the Prado
to be awed once a week by fantasmal
visions from Goya's dark period,
(Saturn Devouring One of His Children)
and both versions of the naked Maja
hanging nonchalantly in a stair well
on either side of a door.

I am told the Retiro park is still safe
and Madrid has purged itself of Franco,
but the town, alas, has lost its *siestas*,
endless *paseos* and dinner at ten—
I still remember *mi direción*;
I would tell the taxi driver,
'Alberto Aquilera Siete—bajo el arco'

A PILGRIMAGE TO CHRIST'S TOMB
(Protestant version)

'*Quem*

quaeritis?'

asked an angel

at the empty tomb,

but I,

too taken

with her translucent linen

and the urge to crush

her ample wings,

forgot the

risen

god

A POSTCARD FROM NASSAU
for William James

Why do the
palatable philosophies
trickle redly from sad men,
echo across damp prison floors,
fall faintly from crosses
and bleeding mouths?

Was it a mistake
that we crept from the ooze
walked on hind legs,
felt divine when we
should have crawled back
to the sustenance of
muddy men?

The Duke came
back here to Nassau
where he will remain
long after the scepter
is in a museum.

Are not pink coral reef,
refined white sand
and lucent blue water
fair exchange for
an impotent tradition?

Certainly the Duke seems
content here in the Bahamas
where life is pleasantly sustained
on tropical fruit and sun.

DOWNTOWN ST LOUIS
ON YOUR BIRTHDAY
for Albert S. Hatcher (1904–1980)

1

years tumble now
like water loosed
from dams
of sticks and mud
in forest creekbeds
that cradled
frail dreams;

these structures
never held long
though the brook
was small
and water
trickled only
mounted slowly
like minutes.

2

now I am like you,
several years back
scurrying to catch up
collecting days
in closets
like clippings
from old papers
yellowing
turning to dust;

in time
I will give up
leave memory behind
in these dilapidated
tenement dwellings,
abandoned redbrick elders
with their gargoyles,
pseudo-Greek colonnade,
and brocade darkened ·
like dried blood.

3

a premature
fall chill
bathes my face,
reminds me how
you are a
part of all this—
honest
charming
formulaic;

I tried to
forget you once,
your anachronistic
penchant for order,
your pained nobility,

but you taught me
all too well
your daily lessons,
reflexes bequeathed
by your Christian
farmer father.

4

Nothing passes
slowly now,
not baseball season
trainrides
circuses
summers;

but here in this
neglected corner
of St Louis
is the perennial hope
of September
because we are
an autumnal clan
bound by zodiacal charts
rooted firmly
in the virgin
whom spring could
never rival
and for our love
and tears.

5

father
these archaic forms
cannot last;
decrees are issued
by the hour,
condemn what is
cacophonous
amid glass and
polished steel;
but your country virtue,
no less conspicuous,
is not so quickly
ruined—
diffused through me
through mine,
this inheritance
guides us through
guideless times.

PART SIX

Waiting for the Prime
After the Prime

For we have wanted to preserve passion and we cherish the unhappiness it brings with it; and yet at the same time both passion and unhappiness have stood condemned in the sight of official morals and in the sight of reason.

Denis De Rougement

WAITING FOR THE PRIME
AFTER THE PRIME
for me on my 29th birthday

I

stopping the sun from cropping up each day
so quickly over my feet through the shades
rose to orange to gold to blinding white

which it becomes each morning
in spite of auspicious beginnings—
that's what I'm about while I still have unplanted

these seeds in my brain like evening stars,
like pebbles, like grains of sand between my teeth,
like an oyster, like the smallest embryo.

I am still waiting like myself
at a distant frosted window listening
for tinkling Christmas bells;

I am still wanting a marriage bed,
untainted sheets unfurled and strings
touched by hands from somewhere I cannot name.

2

The year before last
I exalted my free will
and for a while it was sufficient—

I did not conquer time,
but I lost my father's watch
and cancelled the newspaper subscription.

last year,
last year and this,
nothing is really satisfying,

not fame,
trees, forests, fields
or strange animals;

and the further along I get
and the more astigmatic my eyes,
the more things I trip on

and the harder it is
to remember
exactly why.

3

Today I am
determined once more—
this time to escape all my friends

to go trudging off to the North Woods
where they cannot get at me—
if by chance they really decide to;

today I will discover a place
where mornings shall be
quite different;

instead of dissolving,
the sun will stay
point still,

until it turns me golden;
yes, I will be golden
and rubbed with scented oils,

scented
and praised
for the texture of my skin

though not desiring praise,
not exactly
needing it;

the mornings will be gracious
and the nights
when in time they do approach

will be pensive,
studied,
starlit, wide.

4

These dreams are the seeds I sow
sometimes for you
but mostly for me;

so many years I have sought
some plot of dark earth to sow in
—to sow them all:

not just the red one
or the green one
or the one that tastes like honey;

I would plant them all
like swords,
bury them to the hilt.

RESCINDING:
GETTING MY FALL CHECK-UP

Calculating my choices last spring
I tossed out all my poems sardonically,
shut the eye that spies analogies
every place I pass by,
produces epics from three-second visions;

but now it cranks up again on its own
this mechanism that visits my sleep
with voices, with whole phrases:
Do not, do *not* get emotionally involved
it tells me at my annual checkup.

Myself perched silent on the table end
shirt off, a bit of a paunch slipping over the belt,
myself stooped over slowly raises his weary head,
looks at me straight on disgusted;
it's *that* look again;

once more I am sleeping poorly, uneasy
with the furniture, the pictures, the way
the morning creeps up angularly
over the roof, avoiding my windows
that in summer were so receptive;

I know part of me is missing,
feel it missing like a leg
gone from its socket—
every day after school
I used to climb a great fatheroak

that overlooked the woods,
its limbs the size of other trees
and each a trail to be explored.
No one noticed if I climbed well or poorly
—there were no comparisons.

After an evening walk by the goldfish pond,
the wind threatening to get cold,
the dead grass sprinkled with halfwet leaves,
I remembered my father and how
he always made lists.

Sometimes he tried not to make lists,
but sometimes he made lists of lists.
For so long his life seemed to me
a list instead of a poem;
now my poems are columned like lists.

When my glands took cues from holy writ,
I was a young man to be admired, or scrutinized—
then in her eyes were lives
I didn't expect to see there—
the two of us stretched out

listening to Bach and becoming neo-classified;
my fingers traced patterns in the rug
little roads from my shoulder to her bare arms;
our minutes became palpable friends
until one morning I found myself

kneeling on the floor with tears piecemeal
scraping pride together
vowing solemn oaths to five different gods,
a part of me watching, dispassionate,
smiling, aloof, obnoxious.

After vowing allegiance to father's law
when I fell from a brittle poplar,
I found myself later
(a few minutes later)
midway between the second limb

and the green grass below,
upside-down but already
anticipating his scorn—
I was never good at acquiescence;
I specialized in aspiration.

Child of my dreams, do not stay—
but do not go!
Do not look so pretty, tanned and blond.
Do not lead me so easily into those forest traps;
I would be more than your brief mirror.

A REFUSAL TO DROWN EASILY

approaching your time
seconds well up
from belly to throat

palpitate slower, rounder,
each one
rounder than the last

I depend on you depend on me
and we are caught
in circuities

we are caught
by a southwest wind
in our faces

and cannot turn back
(the wind would be
awkward at our backs)

southwest we walk toward thickets—
out of the sun
and curious eyes

we are caught
in tree limbs
playing with the sun

and the wind making
patterns on your face
and in your hair;

the manner of our lips
says more than the words
and always our eyes

are transparencies
and always your eyes
get deeper

always your eyes are open to me,
always your hands,
send messages:

we are good like this
we are more than we expected
we are more than is comfortable.

approaching our time
seconds lodge in my throat
and stop;

unwittingly we are becoming
vignettes strung together
on a string of need;

we wait for some Shaper of Parts
who understands form
to put it all together.

APOLOGIA

At six I was the master of fantasy,
the dramatist supreme,
made a stage on a ping-pong table,
and a throne draped in purple,
cardboard crowns sparkling with carbuncles,
robes of splendid elegance
from father's discarded terri cloth.

I wreathed a banner in lights,
flags went up outside,
and at special invitation
grown-ups put aside daily chores,
reverently descended basement stairs
into the eerie light of my theater
waited patiently in folding chairs,
politely applauded as I ascended
with scepter and orb in hand;

I sat above them red-faced—
having forgotten to write a play—
giggled nervously,
rocked back too far,
crashed onto the concrete floor,
got sympathy enough for a swollen head,
but no accolades.

I was like that today,
but surely you knew I meant
much more.

THE ALBATROSS
AROUND MY NECK

That inescapable animal walks with me,
Has followed me since the black womb held,
            Delmore Schwartz

        The magnificent
            gooney bird
                glides
                    down

    fetishly
            as stabbed through,
                spreads umbrellas
                    popelike

    to bless
            the wind
                not scratch
                    the sand.

    He is my
            brother—
                ever aspiring
                    to grace,

        sailing
            so sure,
                balanced on
                    that air

    until at the
            last second
                he tumbles
                    tail

    over
            beak into
    a
        feather
    ball.

TRANSCOPEDIMANIPULATION

i sit here
rubbing your foot
while you rub mine;

there must be
a word for this
properly derived
from Greek
or Latin roots
with prefixes
and suffixes
to place you
there
your eyes
sensual and
smiling,
me here
almost asleep;

somewhere
this must be
forbidden!

WATCHING FROM YOUR WINDOW

. . . when the fire of love is ablaze, it burneth to ashes the harvest of reason . . .
The steed of this Valley is pain; and if there be no pain this journey will never end.
                                                                Bahá'u'lláh

the day stops in frozen shadow
mute grey passionless sky

the few leaves left are dry
twist in dull color on withered stems

the slate roofs are gothic
and the wind churns a scalded voice

up from the street below—
a child, a dog, a distant hearse.

It is time again for waiting
my brow against this cold pane

time again to listen
in this window seat above the city

for the echo of your footfall
on the stairs or in the hall.

AUBADE

'O, swear not by the moon, the inconstant moon'

Silhouetted by the sunrise,
your hair is gilded, skin tinted brown;
you whisper, 'There is an ebb and flow . . .'

And because your voice is music
I nod in accord while I study
the slope of your neck

the delicate shape of your mouth.
Coots chatter, scud across the sound,
cattails rustle in the wind;

water barely laps the shore
and on my neck I feel
the pull of the moon rising behind us.

You say, 'I must be careful!'
I say, 'So must we all,'
and you sing a song to the moon.

YOUR HANDS

Your hands cupped around mine are pensive.
I cannot see them or whether you watch mine
or like me see only headlights slicing the dark.

We have run out of words today;
only the salt on our skin remains
from our joust in the wind,

waves rocking the white sheets,
cold pricking our skin
precisely firm.

The icy sea made us numb then giddy
and at the quaint cafe we celebrated victory
and ate smoked mullet.

You were an emblem of the day
in your burnished sea-blown hair
and coffee smile;

I would have been your lover,
father, brother—
whatever you wanted.

The tire hum hypnotizes,
the steady moon rises,
glides behind trees;

our hands are all there is.
Did I ever tell you Petrarch disgusts me?
Frauendienst! Frauendienst!

God save me from that—courtesy, courtesy,
the servicing of ladies
the religion of love, the death of communion,

I will not pay homage to heathen deities . . .
Is your hand sending messages?
Should I answer?

Should I spill out my life,
throw myself at your mercy
like a shadowy courtier?

I feel my blood ticking away;
I feel the pounding of a myth
rising deep within me.

No need to say you aren't your smile,
that you curl up
in safe warm places;

your hands say it all—
have not the guile of eyes
the ambiguity of words

leak through these silences
into mine
as the day ends in spite of us.

THE GIRL

who signed my highschool book
to say her love would never die
is now the mother of two
not mine, not knowing my name,
though she and I would sometimes lie
deathly still and swear eternal oaths
in dark and secret places.

GIVE ME BACK MY YOUTH
AND I WILL GRACE IT

Her face was Renaissance
—eyes cow brown,
forehead high,

hair morena,
voice a whisper,
history simple:

one lad had tried,
failed—
knew not why.

Virginal we walked
spoke poems,
we thought,

about the twisted trees
about the squirrel lady
who sat each day

beneath an elm
to feed, she thought,
her babies reincarnate.

we agreed
she was lonely,
just lonely,

our hands
almost touching,
a mist hovering the pond.

The old lady
has long since
abandoned her bench,

the squirrels are
quite on their own,
but I would know now

how to extoll
those iridescent eyes
and mourn that dying afternoon.

PART SEVEN

Tunnel Vision

For the mythological hero is the champion not of things become but of things becoming; the dragon to be slain by him is precisely the monster of the status quo: Holdfast, the keeper of the past. From obscurity the hero emerges, but the enemy is great and conspicuous in the seat of power . . .

Joseph Campbell

TUNNEL VISION

At thirty I woke up
grasping for the headboard
sheets soaked,
heart stopped,
breath sucked in
with a gasp—

I had seen something
unbelievable—
my life an old man's formula,
days replicated
to the edge of doom
like the endless images of myself
in those dressing room
mirrors.

I stumbled to the desk,
its drawers
crammed to the brim
with policies
to ward off blight,
catastrophic illness,
and every unnatural act
of nature;

the plots were selected,
the black suits laid out;
there was nothing more to do
but drive again
the practical car
the way it knew by heart,
chanting to myself as solace
a litany of unasked questions
about the perilous
American Dream.

LATE FALL IN TAMPA

The tropic tune is hummed in silent quartos
pitched low to numb sensibilities
until some bedtime musing one notices
years stepped by without leaving tracks;

no snow cleansed rooftop and fields,
no spring crept in on furry feet,
no fall bellowed torpedos of recognition;
days and seasons rename, repeat themselves.

Before it is recast in the tropic mold,
the mind cycles with time
despite a world gone out of kilter,
but in the third year one must leave or die

with school days, childhood, old sweethearts;
it's painless enough—three changes of clothes
the anesthetizing warmth
that never really leaves the sand;

sometimes at night when the wind
springs loose upon salted streets
remembrance is pricked like a tearing eye
but by mid-morning the sun has beat down passion.

Right now in Nashville the leaves in Centennial Park
are yellowing, coloring bright where once
I made a bed upon the moss
when the day was cold and still;

here there's only rain or no rain,
only hot or mild;
spring relieves us from nothing
but we cannot celebrate February;

associations fade, footings crumble
into fragile lace, settle to a fine powder.
Still, leaving is easier to say than do
when I have given to the Salvation Army

all my winter garb but one strange coat,
and as the third year whirs quietly by,
resolve softens warmly
like unused muscle fiber.

A QUIET TIME
WITH CREDIT CARDS

sitting in
a common stall
doubting that
nirvana is imminent,
I slide
the leathered pouch
from its pocket home
count
the laminated trophies
of my progress through
the years,
compute my gaiety
and grin

MY BRIEF BOUT WITH AMNESIA

yesterday
i forgot
where i live

so i called
a yellow cab
and went to the depot;

from there i travelled
all over the country,
not searching, actually;
just enjoying the sights.

i ended up
out West
lying beside
the Grand Canyon
waiting in vain
for the birth
of God

a monstrous
head
to push through
from the cavernous
river bed.

MIDNIGHT TRIP TO BLACK RABBIT'S CAGE

Because we live in the suburbs
and can't afford a whole brood,

the rabbit has no mate,
must sleep alone in a wire cage

exposed to the dank night air,
and the reason I am

sneaking out right now
with a flashlight to see him

is to discover if he's gotten used to
the solitude.

If he has,
I must know his secret;

If not, I'll stroke his satin ears
till he falls asleep.

DIVORCE

I

The young man flying from his motorcycle
at the busy intersection this afternoon
should fit into my apartment, on my shelves,
or in my closets with other scattered debris,

his eyes studying the melting sunset
his mind climbing dunes on one wheel,
peripherally aware of chrome reflections
from a Continental bearing down head on.

In an instant his mind exploded into stars;
he floated backward upside down and
his helmet bowled curbward, then still.
'So much rubber toy!' my boy gasped sucking air.

The woman driver will always be screaming;
when she is not screaming
she will be prepared for the scream;
she is transmogrified.

Beautiful as Daedalus' vanity was the lad's presumption,
sailing out of reach, making this instant metamorphosis that
lurks around our city corners
as near to me as to my aging father.

He told us more as he half-gainored from the road
than he had ever said to anyone before,
to each of us transfixed at the red light,
as when the first heralding snow hits town

and fitful winds sweep village streeets
skinning limbs of trees for frosting
and some thin coat of urbanity is also shorn;
so sat we in our silences there

watching him sail more strangely than
any bird or beast that we had ever seen.
We might have ambled off the roadside gathering,
gradually discovering what it meant,

but we were closedoored and steelencased;
our climate was controlled and the radio tunes
and dancing neon signs assured us
there was no death nearby, and perhaps it's true—

at that same corner tonight I found no hint
of mortality, no piece of glass bigger than my thumb;
yet as he faded from us today we all heard him say,
'I am dying more dead than you have ever seen.'

We say our house was never really a home;
it had the guise of home—at times it did—
the warmth, the glow, the nurture of a womb,
but go to our house and you will find no home there.

The whole world sings at night out under the moon
when the last TVs are off and streets are quieter;
the lyrics drift in like sea fog over our backyard fences.
They say, 'You will learn only one thing well,

but it will be driven into your brain
like silver needles.'
I hear this only when I go out by myself
late and away from the street lights,

but today the same song pitched high above the car radio,
set my eyes back and hands to face, hung my mouth,
jolted my ears with tympany of flesh on steel.
It required all that young man's skill

to be heard even faintly above the shrill clamor,
but for that instant he was unmistakably clear,
and not as a highway safety slogan; he sang,
'I am dying more quickly than a smile can bleed.'

II

The Picasso on my wall,
a triangular family
from his blue period,
says it all concisely:

only the small boy
has hands
only the small boy
has eyes—
the mother, the father,
their heads bowed
in cold or shame

neither see nor touch
each other nor the
small boy who reaches
out his empty hands
towards them both—

he is asking a question
and all lines converge
at his heart because
he sees but does not
understand;

Last night I woke
screaming after
watching my son
reach for the high
limb in the sweet gum

glide down
then crash like
a porcelain clown.

III
(after-math)

Your father's words
hang about this room
like the too-sweet smell
of his cherry-blend tobacco.
His pipes are racked tight
but he is here more now
than ever he was in flesh,
cursing my youth with clenched mouth,
wounded as he was by my unkind
rhetoric about the holy war
he waged in the Pacific for me
who had stolen your affection.

'He'll be bald before thirty!'
he warned you happily.

My hair outlived him,
though I have scars,
each with a name,
a chart to show precisely
where things went wrong—
and now I understand
that wicked laugh he had,
the cynical edge of it;
I know why the poet in us
must die so young:

It is best so—
after love's sweet pain,
after the scent of your
just-washed hair,
after the half-sleep and
the one aubade that mattered,
after all the furniture
is finally divided up,
what lyrical is left to say?

SUNBATHERS:
AN EXPERIMENT IN
TIME LAPSE PHOTOGRAPHY
for Dr. John Ott

I

the girls in the grass
are dying in the sun
turning brown like dead grasses.

their meaning eludes me
but something more than tempting
stretched out white, untouched

more than letting days
roll over their thighs
imprinting hours in colors:

soon they will not bare waists
spread legs before winter's sun
will want their own taut skin.

2

I quit smoking first by degrees
then all at once
when I felt my lungs darkening,

some haggard bitch grab my chest
and squeeze from inside;
now these girls seize my eyes

like sepulchral nymphs,
they jolt my crooked spine
with their time enough to waste away;

but not far beyond their green vision
lies the specter
of almost fled thews.

3

The girls in the grass
have died so warmly
I cannot notice their passing.

when one goes
and another takes her place;
one long motion bears them all

along the crest of grasses
churning toward a shore stopped still
at a white stone wall

where the grass girls' youth
lies stillborn beside them
on the lakeside field.

A MORNING PRAYER

. . . he whose words exceed his deeds, know verily his death is better than his life.
Bahá'u'lláh

I

Standing on the stonegrey parapet alone,
his haunted eyes peering down night's throat
Macbeth whispered, 'there would have been a time
  for such a word'

but of course there never is.
Even now a part of me is droning that same refrain
to my anxious arms, legs, and groin:

there will be a time and a time and a time . . .
And it's all quite silly,
a game we played as children

straining at long breezy summer afternoons
that sat there pleading
to be filled with us.

2

Watching the forest meander across the fields
his own quick words come to cut him down,
he would have known so easily

had he not tossed away honesty
as he might brush a bug from his armour,
that there would never be a better time.

His death would have become him then
and his last words, no quotable musings
about the endless file of minutes and days;

he would have plucked the moment by its dripping roots
nestled it gently in his hand and formulated
tender eulogies for his nerve-wracked queen.

3

Standing there in time and space
staring out beyond the creeping trees
before the call to alarum

before his mind befuddled with military stratagems
to stave off the inevitable,
he briefly knew that it was as good a time as any.

In that milli-second the truth tiptoed into view
like some quaint and curious beast,
but unseemly, not at all what he wanted it to be.

So he bellowed out his brief axioms
at no one in particular,
brandished his steel-tipped arm to buy some time.

4

Mornings at the mirror I study myself
wondering if with enough sleep
I will have become young again

and always I am surprised
by the wasted stranger standing there;
always I am disappointed.

I study you at night in my poems or on our walks;
I try to make you understand
but never really can;

and it's so insane just to stand there
looking at you coming nearer
or me, or the trees.

MY FEARS ABOUT THE AFTERLIFE
for Keebie 1937–1987

Others who experience this unpleasant 'limbo' state have remarked that they had the feeling they would be there for a long time. This was their penalty for 'breaking the rules'.

Raymond Moody, Jr.

I

sparse snow
came in whispers
clung against the panes
peeked in curious
to see him sitting there
with no face
mute
a finished mime.

it had all come to this
and only this—
the enmeshed rituals,
tangles of days
rattling against
the roof of his mind;

his tin thoughts cadenced;
a lone windmill
chattered in one ear;
a split rail fence
off to the side
stood stacked
like crossed fingers:

2

The aging son
of a fishmonger
who had seen prison camps
from the inside
had told him
how such things happen;

it was he who had said
about the guards
they didn't know
exactly what they were doing
as day after languishing day
amid half-jokes
and coffee breaks
they trudged the wagons
of white stretched bones,
piled higher lacy mounds
and turned to ask offhand
how's the wife?
what's for lunch?

the fishmonger's son
forgives
like spring forgives
to become sane
one day at a time,
says that God forgives
because He must.

But at night late
surely one guard turned on his side
muttered to his Frau
this thing is not for doing;
in the morning he felt himself
his conscience's toy,
determined to stop
the quibbling;

137

daily skin and bone
became only weight
on the cart wheels;
hands, hair, eyes
jostling at gulleys
in the routine mud track
cropped up sometimes
in dreams
then remitted;

those hollow bulging sockets
brimming with humanity
became in time
only eyes.

watching the snow
through frozen panes,
he saw no forgiveness
in the skinned trees
no facile grace to sever
that shimmer through the universe
to dissolve the garish apparition
of the deed's vicar.

back in the pitch of youth
behind Aunt Cynthia's
white frame farm house
looking out from a hayloft door
in Franklin, Tennessee,

he owned a name
that rhymed with a flower,
swore to devote himself
entirely to the works
of the Lord—

        if John Wesley
could have
an epiphany at Aldersgate,
then so could he in Tennessee;
had not God already
saved him thrice from fire?

Cousin Keebie had been
of the same mind
when they made a summer pact,
ran down the green knoll
full force toward
the Harpeth River,
leaped the low scrub bush,
missed the large rocks,
the legs barely able to keep up,

rolled the last yards
in a swelter of giggle,
plunged headlong into
that muddy, sanctified
water.

4

larger flakes
fell like holy wafers;
up close, fine webs of ice,
no two the same—

as witting deeds
had sliced so quickly
the knotted covenants
sworn under the stars
or lying in bed with
the good book warm on his chest,
and the archaic words hanging there
oddly mingled with pity and fear
hovering above like chiding friends;

he could not now
return the knife to Old Man Haver's store
untell the lie how he'd got it
uncoerce the good soldier friend
unremember the haunting
that promptly lost the three blades
and leather punch
weeks later in compliance
with Freudian law;

but from then on,
he had determined,
it was all going to be
quite different.

5

To have again
such simple tricks,
he thought
as the snow in clumps
filled the glass up
and trees faded
to faint lines;

or to be
Thomas Mitchell,
the cinematic old salt
lying at night
on the ship's deck
dying repentant
in his mate's arms,
smiling at the last
as he looks past
the grieving friend,
a bewildered Clark Gable;

he stares up and out
into the laden sky,
reaches for his
immortal soul,
catches instead
a shooting star,
smiles and rides
to peaceful sleep.

6

But oh how long to wait
till the earth turns
one degree at a time
minute by minute
hour by hour on axis
until some forgiving
thaw?

And how long
if to sit only,
to wait and watch
and see nothing
but what the window sees,
to feel nothing
but what the tree
in its dwindling bark
feels?

Not to move
or to need to move,
to stare and wonder
if this is the year
the works get stuck
in ice.

PART EIGHT

Waiting for America

> how all
> the agonies of our deathbed childbed age
> are process, major means whereby,
> oh dreadfully, our humanness must be
> achieved.
>
> *Robert Hayden*

TAKING A BIRD APART

nestled
in my hand
a bird
waits;

its feathers
are red and blue
tinged with white
and I pull them
from its wings
one by one;

they slide out
painlessly
and the bird
is patient,
motionless.

last night
this was the
perfect metaphor
and I can't
remember
why.

DR. WILL AND THE
DEATH OF HARMONY GROVE

A Portrait of William Benjamin Hardman (1865–1918)
as told by his brother, Thomas Colquitt Hardman

He was the fourth son born—
just ten days before Lee's surrender—
in the old home place on Madison County Road;
there his father practiced medicine
for the hard-working folk
around Harmony Grove, Georgia.

He was most fond of dogs as he grew up,
stayed with old Rat the hound
when father made him sleep on the porch
if he got too impudent or rowdy at night—
a punishment, Pa said.

But years later no one was surprised
when I hitched up Kate
to take irrepressible young Will
off to Mercer college—
he had always been good in math,
and a ready debator,
won the hundred yard dash
and standing broad jump, too.

Oh, he was a dandy all right—
combed his hair to a nicety
made his toilet of heliotrope
or attar of rose.
Slender and tall he was,
went to Mardi Gras in 1886
and gave the Valedictory Oration—
in Latin!
        Pity no one knew
what he said—it had to do with
the glorious destiny of America.

Yes, quite the dandy,
if not a masher
for the dignified 80s

and gay 90s
in his derby hat, button shoes,
his frock coat, pin-striped pants,
silk umbrella, and Prince Albert coat
with satin lapels!

In 1887 he was off to New York,
the College of Physicians and Surgeons,
and he saw before him a world
that was dying just as another
was being born:

Bell and the telephone,
the Vanderbilts with their railroads
criss-crossing the land,
Edison and his electric lights.

Will told me that summer
home from school
he would rather live
fifty years in the twentieth century
than twice that long any time else.

Well, the good Lord didn't give him that,
but he used the time he had—
like Achilles, I always thought.

He came back here to Harmony Grove
in the spring of '89,
bought the town paper in '91,
(wrote the editorials himself),
bought the drugstore too,
changed it from wood to brick.

There was no stopping him—
president of the phone company,
then the bank,
bought up farms left and right—
planted peach orchards:
for a while the biggest landowner
in the whole state.

But medicine was his true love.
He and brother Lamertine
built the town a first-rate clinic
complete with an operating room.
Yet Will was a religious man,
superintendent of the Baptist church.

But let me tell you,
when he drove that bright red
1911 Baby Maxwell
on the streets of Harmony Grove,
it was the first car most had ever seen,
and a hush would fall—

Will with his trim moustache,
eyes so deep they seemed
to stare right through a body,
and all the ladies would whisper,
'There goes Dr. Will!'

Then to everyone's surprise,
he built this home in the center of town,
here on little Pine Street
for his bride Ida Shankle—
It was out of place,
this huge columned mansion
among these small frame houses,
but Will told me,
     'Thomas,
let's make this town into
something fine and proud
and modern!'

That's when he got the idea
to change the name of Harmony Grove
to 'Commerce'—
so things would happen here,
not of cotton and orchards only,

not just another mill town,
but art and symphonies
rows of townhouses
and no one having to do
without.

He got the name changed all right,
but no one except Dr. Will himself
really understood what he had in mind
because they hadn't seen what he'd seen—
if Will thought it a good idea,
that was enough for them.

And who could blame them—
a life like his, so full
we cannot now conceive it,
and his heart so pure
we still long to imitate it,
and his motive so right
he was elected mayor against his wishes.

Of course, in 1918 the flu was about
and his heart had not been sound
since Ida's death in childbirth;
but his duty was so strong
that he left that last cold October night
in the thick of rain in a buggy
pulled by the long-legged grey mare
he loved so much—
and all to set a young boy's leg.

That's how the house got built here,
and that's how the name got changed.
True, brother Lam got elected governor,
but without Dr. Will to guide it along,
Commerce just sat biding its time,
waiting for the century to come to its doorstep.
I tell you, a life like his is all too brief.

THE AWFUL WONDERS OF THE SUN BAY TOWERS DEVELOPMENT FOR SENIOR CITIZENS

I am told by several friends that there is, neatly on the wall of each cubiculum in the looming white monument to mercantility rising before me, a door two feet square, coalbin-hatch size, stainless steel, hinged at the top, connected to a chute so when pains come tingling up the arm, one simply leans forward from the waist, then it's zoom down the slide to the basement and plop in the red velvet box on rollers tripping the lid shut—the momentum carrying the whole assemblage (me inside) into the back of a dark waiting Cadillac, station-wagon-shaped, motor running.

ROY ROGERS
CONTEMPLATES IMMORTALITY

first there was Trigger
(horses die younger)

and now standing
statuesque as ever

the beast must feel
from deep within

some taxidermical remains
that art is life inextricably—

the palomino in him unchanged;
now Dale crumbles,

no longer sustained by straps
paints and sutures;

she awaits those clever hands,
anticipates her place supreme

on the front yard pedestal,
higher than the horse,

her eyes hazy blue aggies,
her smile quaintly fixed;

she will reign magnificently,
cowgirl platonized eternally.

TENT MEETING
AT CONYERS, GEORGIA

Arm in arm they pace the hill
past grass-filled hulks of cars
file in rhythm to hear his Southern mouth
pour out some Sunday steam.

As they sit, rock in caneback chairs,
he whips up red clay dust,
shakes the ground beneath them,
thunders their chests from inside.

'Lawd, *Lawd*!' one shouts.
'Like a trillion blackbirds overhead!
Do you feel his power in you?
Just like old Jesus, I betcha!'

SIXTEEN SECONDS BETWEEN
GROUND ZERO AND
SAMARA DRIVE

Saturday afternoon at 4.35 and fifteen seconds
found Herman spraying lethal gases
at pesky chinch bug masses
eating unsightly patterns in his lawn.

It was a hard-to-keep-up-with neighborhood
even with the right tools
all properly labeled and arranged
on a pegboard wall in the garage.

So when the earth sucked in at ground zero
and the immediate area puffed up from the wound
only Herman noticed on Samara Drive—
big game on TV.

Quite certain of what it meant,
Herman felt an odd relief,
stopped his work, leaned upon the edger
he was using to manicure his drive,

and sighed like an old farm hand
pausing while revitalizing his garden sod.
He watched the circle flare up red,
then wreathe out like lightning ripples

on a rock-shattered pond.
From Samara Drive it looked
not quite so crimson as their better sunsets,
nor as high as the brooding thunder heads

the Chamber of Commerce brochure said
were as beauteous a part of the Samara view
as the equi-spaced Queen Anne palms.
But at 4:35 and twenty-five seconds

Herman lay down, his back inclined
against the carpet lawn,
head on hands,
poised between the silent fall afternoon

and the shock wave with its evaporative heat wall.
He stared up and out,
spread his legs a little,
so that as the fire storm reached Samara Drive,

engulfing the elegant Haversham house,
Herman felt pure energy press his thighs,
move across his chest like quilted lead.
He had always loved snow storms,

wind storms, thunder, and flood—
whatever broke the monotony.
So as a palm and part of a porch flew by
at 4:35 twenty-nine

Herman felt himself breathe out,
'I love you, God!'
At 4:35 thirty-one,
Herman's atoms disarrayed,

mingled with sand, houses,
with Havershams,
into a grand orange ball
that broiled up Samara Drive.

MEMO:
ATTENTION ARCHEOLOGISTS
(found scratched on the shard of a
1984 Canon AS-100 word processor)

Though tersely, I chant like blind Homer
cataloguing ships along the shore—
Heinrich Schliemann's dreamcometrue
in the solid layers
of nine different Troys—

like the *scops* in high-beamed halls
who doled out golden *beahs* of verse
as recompense for mighty handgrip
to retainers highminded and resolute—
at Sutton Hoo we even found his harp!

I sing for all of you, reasonable men
divining clues to our sundry paradoxes.
Neither myth nor enigmatic metaphor—
we really marched like this,
lock step to the brink of a globeless world

and beyond . . .

BECCA

> *If only I could nudge you from this sleep,*
> *My maimed darling, my skittery pigeon.*
> *Over this damp grave I speak the words of my love;*
> *I, with no rights in this matter,*
> *Neither father nor lover.*
>
> Theodore Roethke

Not a week is gone and already it is hard to remember
when this grief did not cast its pall
over all our dreams of life.

there was such speed in her little body

We sit in this country church watching amid cascades of flowers
the different aspects of ourselves,
studying what we mean by this gesture.

and such lightness in her footfall

Monday night it was the lead story on local news—
'a tragedy to mar the opening day of classes,
ten-year-old Rebecca Dye in critical condition.'

it is no wonder her brown study astonishes us all.

By Tuesday morning there were no brain waves
and surgeons with technical hands dismantled her,
parcelled her out as gifts.

Soon the news of her is surpassed by grosser numbers—
a bus hit and six dead,
one miracle child survives from a planeload of 158.

Figures pour in like battlefield reports,
ciphers we use instead of names to trick ourselves
into staying sane each morning at the breakfast table.

Now a hurried final glimpse before attendants close the lid—
Becca in her recital dress—
even here she's playing a part,

Jane Banks in *Mary Poppins* dancing her fantasy in the park,
a painting Seurat would love—
a jolly holiday with Mary . . .

but the strains of 'Abide with Me . . .' signal
that this is not mere choreography;
She will not step out for us.

One by one her school friends recite in tremulous cadences
a litany of remembrance whose clarity
pierces veils of adult euphemism.

I look among our visages so pitifully drawn—
who among us would not gladly flee this world bedecked
with praise bestowed with no motive but exorcism of grief?

And her unfinished dreams—
to go on pointe, to learn her pirouettes?
It must suffice now that we saw her once

dancing her kite across the stage,
flying her feet like little kites,
letting us believe for a moment in that fictive world

where there is justice, order, denouement.
The reverend in bassed eloquence concurs,
bids us weep, weep,

not to judge God's hand in this,
'except', he says, 'except she brought us here together,
the many colors and beliefs of us,

touched all our lives and brought us here to wonder.
And the untimeliness of it?' he muses.
'Who's to say what is timely in this life?

Look how ample she made ten short years.
Have we done more for all our time?'
We stand, follow the brief white casket

toward the hilltop meadow
as dark thunderheads loom behind us in the Florida sky
and wildflowers bend in the heralding September wind.

We do not know where she is leading us,
but we follow if only because we do not wish
to return to our houses and hear her name

said matter-of-factly by commentators—
Rebecca Dye whose tragedy mars
only the opening day of school.

No, we want to stand here a while longer,
call her 'Becca',
share in our silence what we have lost,

because it is more than the ratio
of one over the thousands of children who did not die,
and because we have really come here to mourn ourselves

bereft for now of the hope she had,
have come to pray that these dreary numbers,
the statistics of our vanishing innocence,

will not overtake us,
and if my insurance agent asks, as others do,
'Was that their only child?'

as if we might calculate our grief
by how many of her there are,
we must respond, 'We have none like her.'

She is telling us this,
forcing us to confess it,
that we cannot compute our chances

in the sky or on the streets
with actuarial charts, by building houses behind walls,
or sheltering guilt with the symbology of numbers.

Standing here graveside we know,
if only for this instant,
that for each faceless digit on the nightly news

there is a life touching other lives,
binding us all together in the common war we wage
to save what we hold dear about ourselves.

PART NINE

A Sense of History

The time fore-ordained unto the peoples and kindreds of the earth is now come. The promises of God, as recorded in the holy Scriptures, have all been fulfilled. Out of Zion hath gone forth the Law of God, and Jerusalem, and the hills and land thereof, are filled with the glory of His Revelation.

Bahá'u'lláh

A SENSE OF HISTORY

. . . when I find myself in Chicago and when, travelling northwards out of the city, I pass the Bahá'í temple there, I feel that in some sense this beautiful building may be a portent of the future.

Arnold Toynbee

I

The government photographer
went everywhere to record
the ascendancy of the Qájár kings
over the obstinate sect
that refused *taqíyyih*,
but the camera would not lie.

Badí' the wonderful one
kneels placidly
left hand cupped in reverence
right hand at rest
on his robed thigh
like an aged yogi
surrounded by an entourage
of obedient initiates;

his mouth is firmly set,
his eyes grimly peaceful—
one hardly notices
the huge chain links
around his young neck
grasped at either end
by captors
          who seem troubled
as if they'd rather be
somewhere else,
beside a country stream,
tending an afternoon
samovar;
          they know
there is something
odd in all this.

Wearing his shackles
like a medallion of honor,
Badí' knows as he stares
into the government lens,
peering not at them
but at me now,
that he is saying
more with that glance
than he might have scribbled down
in hours of final haste.

It is all right,
he is saying to me—
I was chosen for this moment.

With the sudden mallet's crash
he leaves the bewildered
farráshes standing there
empty-handed.

2

Crosslegged
beside his beautiful
Rúḥu'lláh
sits Varqá the poet
Varqá the martyr
Varqá the Dove.

Almost a smile
upon his lips,
he senses his son's support,
prodigious strength
in those twelve years.

Strung side by side
like waiting game
they gaze through
that magic window
into my eyes
into my most hidden heart.

This is for you,
they are saying
in that moment before
the Dove is slashed
and the youth must give
his fatal answer
alone.

3

The camera also caught
the dashing emperor's eye;
he is framed in elegance,
seated just so in the family chair—
his face at a royal angle
sword in lap
shoes finely polished
his moustache
waxed and twirled;

he has just issued
lethal commands
is certain the matter is
finally closed,
the Qájár line secure
against upstart remnants
who had thought to usher in
an age of peace;

his eyes are flat
dull, hollow,
doomed now to the
hallway entrance
of a mansion outside Akka
where daily they must
watch without reprieve
a chorus of portraits
on the opposing wall
bloom in bouquets
of smiling faces,

descendants of those same
haunting visages
he had thought to slaughter.

They don't see
him watching—
they never did.

THE PRIMAL POINT

I am the Primal Point from which have been generated all created things . . .
The Báb

Near dawn the city of Shiraz sleeps
while in an upper room of a modest house
a young Mullá sits in quiet ecstasy

watching his host, a young Siyyid,
guide ceaselessly a pen across grateful pages,
unmasking the allusive Surih of Joseph

fulfilling this final test
for the enthralled student of Siyyid Kázim
who has ached for yet not dared expect this moment.

As the beatific voice intones the lucid image
of truth behind ecclesiastic veils—
Joseph as Prophet, the Prophet as beloved

and the long-lost Brother about to be found—
Mullá Husayn feels within his humble throat
Gabriel's voice stirring long lost tribes

from centuries of relentless sleep:
'Awake, for, lo! the morning Light has broken.
Arise, for His Cause is made manifest.

The portal of His grace is open wide;
enter therein, O peoples of the World!
For He Who is your promised One is come!'

Now is the time, the time of the end,
Now is the time of judgment,
Now is the point of true beginning.

The voice stops as the morning sun
pierces stained glass;
the dawn call of the adhan summons the faithful,

and the thread of every life
becomes entwined into one lovely
and variously colored cloak.

MULLÁ ḤUSAYN

With this historic Declaration the dawn of an Age that signalizes the consummation of all ages had broken.

Shoghi Effendi

Heeding purest instinct, he has come
from Karbilá to discern the timeless face of God
in the countenance of a courteous young stranger;

Thus does he enter the Kaziran gate,
and himself becomes the Bábu'l-Báb
—Gate unto the very Gate.

When the Surih of Mulk is finished,
Mullá Ḥusayn calmly sets aside
his plaintive longing and priestly titles,

abandons at once the tantalizing search,
to become teacher, warrior,
whatever the time requires,

whether the long trek to Tehran,
a fateful letter by his side,
or whether to his native Mashhad

where in the Bábíyyih he will
welcome in the wakened ones,
or else in a moment of truth outside

the makeshift walls of Fort Ṭabarsí
he will with literal sword act out for us
the unyielding power of certitude.

THE GARDENS OF BADA<u>SH</u>T

*[The Báb's] followers, under the actual leadership of Bahá'u'lláh, their fellow
disciple, were . . . in the hamlet of Bada<u>sh</u>t, abrogating the Qur'ánic Law,
repudiating both the divinely-ordained and man-made precepts of the Faith of
Muḥammad, and shaking off the shackles of its antiquated system.*

Shoghi Effendi

The blade of Quddus hovers
above the bare neck of Qurratu'l-Ayn,
solace of all our eyes;

The shocking beauty of her unconcealed face
has caught us by such surprise
as we sit rehearsing our new names

barely dry upon the pages of brief lives,
Fáṭima herself returned unveiled!
Surely this is our judgment!

Our wills like swords hang above
the pathway of all our choices.
Dare we, like her, even now

in joyful abnegation sever
all our pleasant histories,
all we have struggled to become?

In reflex to effrontery
to the heaven of his faith,
'Abdu'l-<u>Kh</u>áliq places knife against his throat,

but Ṭáhirih, undaunted,
in unequivocating tone proclaims
that the time for words has passed:

'I am the word which the Qá'im is to utter,
the Word which shall put to flight
the chiefs and nobles of the earth!'

The face of Quddus quickly softens,
the feigned anger dissolves
and he sheathes a sword whose time will come.

Is it this garden we are in
whose vernal beauty so emboldens us
that we can shed our lives like skin

or is it the power we sense
in the piercing eyes of the raven-haired youth
Whom God will manifest in His own good time?

IN HIS NAME, THE CONCEALER
Tabríz, 1850

*And whensoever the portals of grace did open, and the clouds of divine bounty did
rain upon mankind, and the light of the Unseen did shine above the horizon of
celestial might, they all denied Him and turned away from His face—the face of
God Himself.*

Bahá'u'lláh

I

The ghostly Greek had long ago
assured his faithful charges
no man does evil in full knowledge.
How could they not assent?
Who would wittingly maim his own soul?
But he watches the crowds gather again,
chattering like starlings.

They perch on rooftops,
peer from windows;
fathers hoist their sons high
to see what tricks the condemned Siyyid-i-Báb
might do this time to escape
the imperial farman.

Columned soldiers take aim
at the blissful youth, Anís,
anesthetized by love
strapped like a foetus
to the Prophet's heart.

The Náṣíri soldiers are steady
from years of practicing
practicing this common form,
from following, following commands.

2

The Báb had warned the summoning guards.
'Though all the world be armed against Me,
yet shall it be powerless to deter Me . . .'
He comforted the grieving Christian colonel:
'the Almighty is surely able to relieve you.'

Not even Godly magic could move the rest,
not vanished clouds of gunsmoke,
not seven hundred rifles spent and useless,
the promised miracle complete.

Now these other soldiers aim with full intent;
ten thousand pairs of eyes consent;
hosts of heaven quiver
at this hallowed spot in time,
the judgment of humankind
come round again.

A hush as His lips part—
they listen for the resounding of his mortality,
but hear instead their own requiem:

'The day will come when you will have recognized Me;
That day I shall have ceased to be with you.'

An instant left for free will
before worlds shatter
before sacred tablets tremble
and ingratitude once again reverberates
                              like rifle shots.

3

No, this is not the prodigality of youth,
the timeless will of children
to vex their father's peace
to flood a mother's prayers with tears;
these are grown men playing this child's game;
their decrees are worded carefully;
their weaponry is real.

Peering from the abode of pure abstraction,
the sad Philosopher King watches the gruesome rite
become now the liturgy of 'holy' men;
he recalls the bitter taste of hemlock,
and wonders when knowledge will at last come full.

ṬÁHIRIH
1852

I am preparing to meet my Beloved.
Ṭáhirih

Like a bride
I have been waiting—
perfumed, anxious;
here is a kerchief
to serve your need

now that I have laboured
through villages and vineyards,
bestowing the gifts I had,
trumpeting messianic tidings,
verses I exhaled like lovers' sighs.

And when I held
the infant Master on my lap,
I could dream the future
in his bright eyes.

But, oh,
such sacrifice I saw,
carnage strewn through village streets
as boon for unrecanted faith;
and my own sweet babes,
unaware of priorities
days like these demand
will never understand
          my leaving.

Do your worst, then,
gawking there,
head cocked
like a puzzled hound,
dangling my colors
like a party favor,

you who think
to stop my voice
from blazoning down
the corridors of time
until the emancipation
of us all.

ṢUBḤ-I-AZAL
1868

Then I was right in saying that neither you nor I nor anybody else in the world would prefer to do wrong rather than to suffer it. For, of the two, wrongdoing is worse.

Socrates to Polus

Eternity's Morn,
not foredoomed
to fail,
might have become
his name
but aimed
cainlike
brotherward

missed
pierced instead
his own frail soul
fidgets now
at sunrise
staring eastward;

sitting alone
on a Cyprus beach
vainly awaiting
his appointed hour—
already come
and gone—

wonders where
the glory went
the obeisance
of friends
that reverence
he thought to
pilfer.

THE MOST GREAT PRISON
A Sonnet After Visiting Bahá'u'lláh's Cell in Akka, 1973

If you stand beside the doorway at the top of the stairs
exactly where the guards would have stood,
you can see not too far away a woman on a rooftop
where a century ago she would have stood much the same
hanging out her clothes to dry in the Mediterranean sun
and steady breeze that is always blowing in from the sea.
Perhaps the prayers of pilgrims keep her awake
after her meager lunch and just enough time for a decent nap
before she must deal again with her boisterous children
and prepare the evening meal for her beleagured husband
who labors all day in fields that aren't his own.
But one gets used to the constant din of noises
in walled and crowded villages like Akka where eventually
one can become accustomed to almost anything.

SEVEN PICTURES OF THE MASTER

No name, no title, no mention, no commendation have I, nor will ever have except 'Abdu'l-Bahá.

'Abdu'l-Bahá

1853

A nine-year-old boy
—the apple of his father's eye—
waits in a prison yard with Ethiopian servant,
trembles for his Lord and Father to emerge
from putrid dungeon into shocking light.
The wretched line of doomed men stagger out.
His father's head is bowed by weighty links
of the infamous Qará-Guhar chain.
The boy who has heard the word of God
issue forth from his Father's mouth,
studies in horrific grief
the irony of man's inhumanity to God,
renews his vow with every pounding breath
to serve, to serve, always to serve.

1892

After days of anxious waiting,
young Ṭarázu'lláh's petition is finally granted.
At long last he sits at the feet of his Beloved,
not daring to gaze into those amazing eyes.
In an instant Bahá'u'lláh teaches him
the equation of His Covenant:
Have you not been with the Master?
then you have been with Me.

1899

Folk king to the outcasts of Akka,
in whose streets wander the homeless of every land
the Father of the Poor rides to the side of His Beloved
on a white donkey, so lowly but oh so serviceable
in all its blessed meekness.

A few years later in táj and white 'abá
he will say to pilgrims from the West,
who one and all sense His perfection,
that they have come to this humble house
not to witness only but to be anointed:
'Look at me, follow Me, be as I am,'
and indeed like candles they will
weep away their lives to give us now
this pure and radiant light.

1909

Zechariah prophesied it;
now the Branch has indeed built the temple
and the sacred dust finally at rest.
The Servant casts aside His cloak and turban,
bends low over the plain wood sarcophagus,
his silver hair waving about his head.
In ghostly lantern light He places
his forehead on the casket edge,
purges sixty years of secret sorrow
while all about him marvel
at his luminescence.

1913

Like His Father before Him Who ignored
sycophantic amenities to 'Abdu'l-Azíz,
the Master disdains American sitting rooms,
idle teas, visits instead the Bowery Mission,
and in perfect candor says,
'I am in love with the poor!'
The very image of their Savior and Lord,
he shows them how to celebrate their poverty
then asks them one and all
to receive Him as their servant.

1916

The mathematics of His chosen name
confirms the paradox of all his choices:
not *Áqá, Sirru'lláh, Ghusn-i-A'ẓam,*
but servant to the word of God made flesh
and himself fleshing out the words,
as poetry of human possibility
and fortress to those who believe.

1921

He looks up at the holy mountain of Carmel
where the stand of cypress reaches heavenward,
where the Blessed Beauty led him,
pointed a shaking finger at the lowly stones
to anoint earth's axis.
'Now it is finished', the Master sighs,
and leaves one parting gift for Aghsán, Afnán,
for all the friends alike,
a youthful branch
branched from Sacred Trees.

ST PAUL'S VISIT TO ALBERT SCHWEITZER'S JUNGLE MISSION

Let deeds, not words, testify to thy faith, if thou art a man of true learning. Cease idly repeating the traditions of the past, for the day of service, of steadfast action, is come.

Ṭáhirih to Vaḥíd

none of these things
can save you;
you can do nothing
to earn eternal life.

It is not our work that
saves us, but Faith
in the Lord Jesus Christ,

You do not receive Eternal
Life by working for it
or by trying to make
yourself behave.

Doesn't it make sense
to believe the One who
came back from the dead
and trust Him for
the payment of your sins?

He died on a cross
for your sins
and you cannot be saved
by your works
no matter how well intended.

Accept the payment
He has made
for your sins

and you can rest
and be assured
you have
Eternal Life.

what i gave up
music and the
praise of
friends.

so i forsook a
little comfort
but not because of
disdain.

some thought
the dissertation
heretical
but it was, after all,
only an exercise.

i suppose
to me it was the
living not the nails
that mattered

so when he
walked among the
lepers and healed
the sick,
His words meant something

to my own life
and that's why i left
and cannot

rest.

THE LOTUS OF BAHAPOUR

Hasten forth and circumambulate the City of God that hath descended from heaven. . . .

Bahá'u'lláh

Rising from the dust of India
petals embossed with sheets of white marble
set in place by humble hands of common laborers
about the routine of their daily work
too poor to comprehend or care
how the sheer power of machines
might do the same task
with the flick of a finger.

For years they have trudged through mud
marvelled as the towering spindled wires
meshed together into spidery frame
like skeleton bones of a leaf
held aloft before sunlight;
they have moved slowly,
one painstaking step at a time,
unaware how each hand-placed stone
fits so perfectly into place.

Day by day a miracle is wrought
from handfuls of earth
and lives like flowers rising in the dust
from seeds Sulaymán <u>Kh</u>án sewed
so long ago on these plains
still trampled by the millions
who glean for shelter and bread.

It is here, here among peasants
the edifice rises like a pregnant stem,
unperceived at first until suddenly
one morning they look up from their labor
to notice something wondrous—
the imminence of bloom
sprung up from earth like a lotus
unfolding petals in a steamy marsh.

But not here only; in other unlikely places
the work goes on quietly a brick at a time;
in a Bolivian jungle village where children
learn to feed themselves on words;
in scorched fields of America's Southland
where descendents of African princes
reascend their rightful thrones,
having kept the faith in humble silence;
in the Dakotas where archaic myths are remembered,
then intoned again around communal fires,
recalled like fluted wavering
from an ancient woodland pipe
whose theme is the ripeness of this time.

SUNBURST

*Out of Zion hath gone the Law of God, and Jerusalem, and the hills and land
thereof, are filled with the glory of His Revelation.*

Bahá'u'lláh

shining from Carmel
slicing gathered clouds
shoots of light reflect

from rocks and clear eyes,
from roses spring-scented
after the elixir bath;

veiled as the Maiden face,
quiet as morning's cool hand,
swift as gone lightning,

the dew-glossed earth glistens,
listens to its parched land
drink deep;

valleys yawn,
sacred streams replenish
after the sudden spring shower.

CORRESPONDENCES
Meditation in the Sequoia Grove at Bosch Bahá'í School in the Santa Cruz Mountains

Know thou that the Kingdom is the real world, and this nether place is only its shadow stretching out.

'Abdu'l-Bahá

The rings on this sequoia become ever smaller
as the years stretch away from the center of its life,
the nascent spirit that drove from the kernel
the hyperbolic tree whose tender bark
muffles our voices in this circular grove.

After quakes and flames strafed San Francisco,
tireless emigrants found out this mountain retreat,
pirated the godlike trees from their massive stumps,
dragged them up the coast to try again
but unwittingly left the roots alive and hidden
mulched and sheltered by neighboring Douglas Fir.

These elders whose ten-foot bases we see
are lost to all but our astounded thought,
though the offspring have reached
a young eighty years or so,
and circle around us here like a wagon train
to protect us, or guard against us.

They exhort us with this mystic shape
like temple walls to ward against
the clamor up the coast—-
did not Brabantio warn the Moor,
'She hath deceived her father, and may thee?'

But here in this unexpected quiet
where deer forage and sunlight filters
into green lace filigree above our heads
we are stunned into mute reverence
at the majesty of holiness writ so large
so unmistakable.

We make a circle of our own, hold hands, and pray:
Save us now, save us for these forests.
O, Guard us now, guard us from ourselves
that we may build in our human hearts
the forms of a world whose shadows we adore.

HAVING ANOTHER CHILD
AT ALMOST FIFTY
for James Varqá Hatcher
(born September 18, 1989)

How is it that with all these years
and my bones beginning to bend perceptibly
beneath the weight of all the lives I have lived
that instead of casting off like nature,
I gather unto me more and more
generations I spawn not at all like beasts
impervious to aught but laws
of survival and satiety?

Because there is love and I
cannot get enough or too much of it
and because eternity's ample maw
will patiently wait the augured hour
when I too must sit only
like the grizzled old men
rocking on crackling porches
in their faded overalls
watching real lives parade before them
on the main streets of their reverie.

GREEN LAKE, WISCONSIN
September, 1988

When we finally achieve the goal of our journey, the end of our search, we can set aside for a while all that has happened along the way.

Rúmí

And so it is that my life
like the seasons has come full circle.

The leaves are laden with color
and the lake burgeoning with steelhead.

Here on this bench at Lone Tree Point
where in the summer of 1888 a sudden storm

drove Mrs. Lawson's boat to this land's end,
addicted her to the promise of peace of mind,

I too find respite on this quiet lawn,
refuge from the life we all would flee.

Gathered here with my friends to celebrate
the covenanted promises of God,

I stroll the shores of this,
the deepest lake in all Wisconsin,

exploring correlatives
for inexorable truths about ourselves

that in these moments we might forge poems
from the tangle of our lives;

for we have assembled here to ask
one unrelenting question—

not about what lies beyond the horizon
where sails evaporate in morning haze,

but only this—
how are we doing so far?

In a church play at age nine,
I was John Wesley struggling methodically

to become truly born again,
and the artifice gave me cause to wonder

if the part might be type-casting,
if I too might some day merit transformation.

And though with effort I still recall
the pitched battles of my heart that followed,

it is as the fiction of a dream,
someone else's life, not mine.

Now my own corporeal shadow
becomes a noisome stranger,

a *memento mori* I keep around to remind me
I am yet imperilled and moribound.

And though I am not Ulysses,
in my secret heart I too hate the shore,

would happily sail out my days
on this deep cold water,

casting my line for only what is needful,
hearing no sound but voices of my children,

my dear wife beside me at the tiller
while I trim the sails.

But this is not a time for leisure.
Soon the wind will sting our faces,

rend the trees of their rainbow harvest
while we prepare for the unkind winter

if we wish to emerge
on the other side in spring,

to creep out of the chrysalis of our becoming,
and a new race after all.

Poems Previously Published

'Afterlife', *Bahá'í Studies Notebook* (Ottawa, 1980), pp. 13–18.

'A Sense of History', *Bahá'í Studies*, Vol. 7 (Ottawa, 1980), pp. 15–17.

'All I Have to Show', *South Florida Review*, 6 (Tampa, Fl., 1972), p. 7.

'A Quiet Time with Credit Cards', *Gnosis*, spring (Brooklyn, N.Y., 1969), p. 20.

'Ariadne's Complaint', *Wisconsin Review*, 3 (Oshkosh, Wis., 1970), p. 7.

'The Awful Wonders of the Sun Bay Towers Development for Senior Citizens', *Foxfire*, Vol. III, No. 2 (Rabun Gap, Ga., 1969), p. 41. Reprinted in *World Order Magazine*, Vol. IX, No. 4 (Wilmette, Ill., 1975), p. 55.

A version of 'Becca', originally appeared in prose as an article in the *Tampa Tribune*, Section B, page 1, September 6, 1987.

'Late Fall in Tampa', *South Florida Poetry Review*, 5 (1971) p. 24.

'Foreknowledge and the True Story of Marvin Rainwater's Remarkable Vision', *Back Door*, 2 (Poquoson, Va., 1970), pp. 47–49.

'For William James', *Poetry Venture*, IV, 1 (St. Petersburg, Fl., 1971), p. 8. Reprinted in the anthology *Poetry Ventured: A Poetry Anthology* (St. Petersburg, Fl., 1972), pp. 6–7.

'A Morning Prayer for Existentialism' originally appeared as 'Macbeth' in *White Mule* (Tampa, Fl., 1975).

'From St Louis on Your Birthday: Albert S. Hatcher, 1904–1980', *Gryphon*, VI, 3 (Tampa, Fl., 1980), pp. 17–19.

'The Girl Who', *Folio*, V, 2 (Birmingham, Ala., 1969), p. 30.

'Great Grandfather's Curious Letters', *South Florida Poetry Journal*, Nos. 4 and 5 (Tampa, Fl., 1970), pp. 130–131.

'Hitchhiking Through the North Georgia Mountains: A Lament for Sidney Lanier', *White Mule* (Tampa, Fl., 1976).

'Inheritance', *Descant: The Texas Christian University Literary Journal*, XIV, 2 (Fort Worth, Tex., 1970), p. 30.

'In His Name, The Concealer: Tabríz 1850', *Abiding Silence: An Anthology of Poems in Honour of the Bahá'ís of Iran. Ed. Shirin Sabri. Bahá'í Studies*, Vol. 15 (Ottawa, 1986).

'Memo: Attention Archaeologist', *South Florida Review*, Vol. 4 (Tampa, 1970), p. 22.

'Midnight Trip to Black Rabbit's Cage', *Folio*, VII, i (Birmingham, Ala., 1971), p. 29.

'My Brief Bout with Amnesia', *Handy Homilies*, I, 2 (Tampa, Fl., 1970).

'Necromancy', *South Florida Poetry Journal*, I, 3 (Tampa, Fl., 1969), p. 29.

'The Passing Train', *Dekalb Literary Arts Journal*, Vol. IV, 1 (Clarkston, Ga., 1969), pp. 46–48.

'Refusal to Drown Easily', *White Mule* (Tampa, 1975).

'Roy Rogers Contemplates Immortality', *South Florida Review* (Tampa, Fl., 1971).

'Saint Paul's Visit to Albert Schweitzer's Jungle Mission', *Arx*, III, 7 (Austin, Tex., 1969), p. 18. Reprinted in 'Recent American Poetry', ed. Robert Hayden, *World Order Magazine*, IX, 4 (Wilmette, Ill, 1975), p. 56.

'Ṣubḥ-i-Azal 1868', *Bahá'í Studies*, Vol. 7 (Ottawa, 1980), p. 18.

'Sunbathers', *South Florida Review*, Vol. 7 (Tampa, Fl., 1973).

'Ṭáhirih', *Bahá'í Studies*, Vol. 7 (Ottawa, 1980), p. 10.

'Taking a Bird Apart', *South Florida Poetry Journal*, Nos. 4 and 5 (Tampa, Fl., 1970), p. 137.

'To the Duke of Windsor', *South and West: An International Literary Quarterly*, X, Nos 3 and 4 (Fort Smith, Ark., 1972), p. 50.

'The Tollund Man: A Definition of the Soul', *Abiding Silence: An Anthology of Poems in Honour of the Bahá'ís of Iran*. Ed. Shirin Sabri. *Bahá'í Studies*, Vol. 15, 1986.

'The Tomb Revisited or Revised', *South and West: An International Literary Quarterly*, X, Nos. 3 and 4 (Fort Smith, Ark., 1972), p. 50.

'Waiting for the Prime After the Prime', *Foxfire*, VI, 2 and 3 (Rabun Gap, Ga., 1972).

Notes

FOREWORD

William Faulkner, 'The Stockholm Address', in *Masterworks of World Literature*. Eds. Everett, Brown, and Wade, Vol. II (New York: Holt Rinehart and Winston, 1965), p. 955.

PART ONE
THEORIES OF HISTORY

H.G. Wells, *The Outline of History*, Vol. I (Garden City, New York: Garden City Books, 1956), p. 3.

EVOLUTION

Bahá'u'lláh, *Gleanings from the Writings of Bahá'u'lláh*. Translated by Shoghi Effendi. Wilmette, Ill.: Bahá'í Publishing Trust, 1950), p. 215.

INHERITANCE

Because Troy was emblematic of a highly cultured civilization, Caesar Augustus commissioned Virgil to write the *Aeneid* to demonstrate how the Roman Empire ultimately descended from Troy *via* Aeneas. Inspired by the success of this poetic enterprize, poets among other western European peoples attempted similar epics to show their descent from the Trojan people (e.g. Britain was supposed to have been founded by Felix Brutus, Aeneas's great-grandson). Mythologically, the fall of Troy resulted from Paris's being bribed by Aphrodite to choose her as fairest among the goddesses, thus infuriating Hera and Athene who conspired to avenge themselves by destroying Troy.

ARIADNE'S COMPLAINT

Lily B. Campbell, *Shakespeare's Tragic Heroes: Slaves of Passion* (New York: Barnes & Noble, Inc., 1963), p. 23.

Ariadne was the daughter of King Minos of Crete and his queen Pasiphae, who became obsessed with an unnatural affection for a bull and thus begat the Minotaur, to whom annual sacrifices of Athenian youth were made. Ariadne promised to help Theseus kill the Minotaur in exchange for becoming his wife (she had fallen in love with him at first sight). Theseus, with Ariadne's help, found his way into the Labyrinth and killed the Minotaur (her half-brother). Together Theseus and Ariadne sailed from Crete, but a few days later Theseus abandoned her as she slept on the shore of the island of Dia, pregnant with his child.

THE BRAIDED ROPE

These terms and this history concern the founding of the Korean martial art of Tae Kwon Do. Archaeological evidence suggests that this art existed as long as two thousand years ago. Based philosophically on the principles of Daoism (Taoism), the techniques of this art were compiled

in 1790 by Yi Deokmoo by order of King Jeongj in the fourteenth year of
his reign.

FOREKNOWLEDGE
Arthur Godfrey was a prominent popular radio, then TV, personality in
America during the 1950s. The people mentioned in this poem were
regular artists on his programs and all became household names. The
setting of the allusion to Odysseus concerns the opening book of Homer's
The Odyssey in which, after some nineteen years away from his native
Ithaca, Odysseus prepares to return. However, in Tennyson's poem
'Ulysses', the hero is not content to live the routine life of a king after all
the exotic adventures he has experienced.

MEDITATIONS AT A PERFORMANCE
Wallace Stevens, 'Peter Quince at the Clavier'.
    1. Giuseppe Guarneri, the greatest violin maker of the Guarneri family,
was a nephew of Andrea Guarneri who had worked with Stradivari.
    2. A French merchant lent Paganini a Guarneri violin to play a concert
(Paganini having hocked his own) and was so impressed by the perform-
ance that he gave Paganini the violin.
    3. After the first performance of the 'Great Fugue', March 21, 1826,
Karl Holz suggested that Beethoven should compose a new Finale that
would be less difficult for performers and listeners alike. Prince Galitzin
had commissioned Beethoven to compose three quartets, of which this
work was supposed to be one, but Holz suggested the work be published
independently.
    4. Bartók discovered what he considered to be authentic Hungarian
folk music and incorporated these themes in his compositions. However,
when the Nazis came to power, Bartók emigrated to the United States and
refused to play this piece either in his homeland or where it could be heard
there so long as his country was occupied by the forces of tyranny.

PROGRESSIVE REVELATION AND THE PROBLEM
OF FREE WILL
Shoghi Effendi, quoted in *Excerpts from the Writings of the Guardian on the
Bahá'í Life*, compiled by the Universal House of Justice and published by
the National Spiritual Assembly of the Bahá'ís of Canada, 1974, p. 4.
    'O Jerusalem . . .' Matt. 23:37.
    'Show us the Father . . .' John 14:8.
    'I am the true vine . . .' John 15:1.

GULL FEEDING
'Abdu'l-Bahá, *Selections from the Writings of 'Abdu'l-Bahá*. Compiled by
the Research Department of the Universal House of Justice (Haifa, Israel:
Bahá'í World Centre, 1978), pp. 80–81.

THE WITAN CONSULTS ON STOICISM (based on folios 88b–89a)
The *witan* ('wise ones') was a counsel of elders or the learned whose
primary function was to advise the king.

Bahá'u'lláh, *The Hidden Words of Bahá'u'lláh*. Translated by Shoghi
Effendi (Wilmette, Ill.: Bahá'í Publishing Trust, 1985), p. 16.

Sometimes referred to as a 'Gnomic' poem, this piece is one of four such
poems extant in Anglo-Saxon. These lyrics have a uniform length and
belong to a genre whose purpose was to recite a composite of axioms about
life, a *de rerum naturum* focused more on social and spiritual principles
than on natural law. While some scholars have viewed these as largely
disjointed observations, it has long been my theory that these poems have
a subtle but exquisite and pervasive unity veiled by their highly symbolic
and metaphoric nature.

'middle dwelling . . .' translates the Old English *middangeard*, which
means literally 'middle place' and designates variously 'earth', 'the globe',
'the world', but derives from the cosmology of the Norse religion wherein
the earth is placed between a celestial abode of the gods and the
underworld which is something like its counterpart in Roman polytheism.

Part Three
GREAT GRANDFATHER'S CURIOUS LETTERS

Julia Ward Howe, 'Battle Hymn of the Republic'. Set to the music of 'John
Brown's Body', this poem first appeared in the *Atlantic Monthly* in February
1862. It became a rallying anthem for the Federal forces in the American
Civil War. Mrs. Howe, an avid abolitionist, later worked for equal rights for
women.

All the poems in this section except for 'Great Grandfather's Curious
Letters' and 'Choosing' are composed largely from letters written by my
great grandfather, Spottswood Henry Hatcher, who was a Confederate
footsoldier in some of the bloodiest battles of the American Civil War. When
a young man, I used to find great pleasure in going to Franklin, Tennessee,
to visit his old homestead where lived his daughter Mary (Great Aunt Mary),
who shared with me his numerous letters and who bequeathed to me his
musket.

ONE FOR MARY JANE
This letter was written when the couple was still courting. They married
six months later on November 29, 1854, and had six children: Mary, John,
William, Henry Thomas, Samuel Andrews, Minnie, and Nanni Lou.

SIGNS OF SPRING
Shoghi Effendi, *God Passes By* (Wilmette, Ill.: Bahá'í Publishing Trust,
1970), p. 151.

Great Grandfather was bivouacked in Tullahoma, Tennessee, not far
from his farm in Franklin. Federal troops ('Yankees') were between him
and home since only a month or so before this letter the bloody battle of

Stone's River had been fought at Murfreesboro (almost 30,000 total casualties—killed, wounded and missing—from both sides). Nevertheless, because of the proximity, he was able to receive some necessities from home—blankets, clothes, food stuffs.

TELL ME ABOUT YOUR GARDEN

Henry Reed, 'The Naming of Parts'.

This letter was also written from Tullahoma during this same period.

'both black and white . . .' Though having only a small farm, they owned several slaves, but as the letter implies, looked upon them not as chattels but as part of the family.

'taking the oath . . .' Southerners living in territory captured by the Federal troops were required to take an oath of alegiance.

A CIVIL WAR

Bahá'u'lláh, Tablet to the Rulers of America, *The Proclamation of Bahá'u'lláh*, p. 63.

'Missionary Ridge . . .' The battles alluded to here took place in the fall of 1863. Though he almost never speaks of what he has seen and experienced, by this time Great Grandfather had been through absolutely horrible battles at Chickamauga (September 19–20th) where there were a total of over 33,000 casualties, and Missionary Ridge (November 23–25th, 1863) where there were over 14,000 casualties. The letter was written in the spring of the following year while the troops were bivouacked at Dalton, Georgia, about two months before the beginning of Sherman's famous advance towards Atlanta which resulted in the battles at Kennesaw Mountain (June 27), Peachtree Creek (July 22), Ezra Church (July 28), and Atlanta itself (August 31–September 1), finally culminating in Sherman's march to the sea (November 15–December 21). The effect of Sherman's attack was devastating to the Confederate forces and heralded the end of the war in the spring.

'Johnson's masterful plan . . .' Johnson had only 55,000 men compared to Sherman's 110,000; he therefore set up a series of nine defensive positions as he retreated towards Atlanta, each one anticipating Sherman's attempts to outflank the Confederate troops. However, Confederate President Jefferson Davis became discouraged with the retreating ploy and replaced Johnson with General John B. Hood, a West Point graduate who had already lost an arm at Gettysburg and a leg at Chickamauga. Though brave and aggressive, Hood was consistently defeated both in Atlanta and later at one of the bloodiest battles of the whole war at Franklin, Tennessee, where my Great Grandfather's own farm became a principal battleground. On the porch of one farmhouse, five dead generals were found. My own father lived for a while in what is called the 'Carter House', a small frame house, now a museum, that served as a command headquarters for the Federal troops.

'old Thomases . . .' A church which still exists and which recently

(June, 1988) honored Great Grandfather's memory with a reunion of his surviving kin.

THE BATTLE OF ATLANTA
Shakespeare, 'Let Me Not to the Marriage of True Minds'.

By the time this letter was written, Sherman's forces had effectively destroyed Atlanta, which had been the railroad center of the South. The city had been burned to the ground (as depicted in Margaret Mitchell's *Gone with the Wind*), and General Hood in a vain attempt to circle behind Sherman's armies, took the forty thousand remaining troops he had north and west up through Alabama. The end result of this maneuver (because he subsequently blundered at Franklin) was the mutilation of his army at Franklin and Nashville. After Nashville, Hood's army was essentially non-existent and he himself asked to be allowed to retire the following month and left for New Orleans where he wrote his memoirs.

'minie balls . . .' a conically shaped musket ball.

SHERMAN'S MARCH TO THE SEA
Sherman did not stop after destroying Atlanta, but without any effective Confederate resistance marched to Savannah, living off the land and laying waste to every structure that stood in the way of his army, thus effectively cutting the South in two and destroying what was left of its morale.

DESERTION
Wilfred Owen, *'Dulce et Decorum Est'*.

Many Confederate soldiers would take unofficial leave of absence to go home and see their families or to plant their crops. Others were able to pay someone to take their place. It would seem from his letters that Great Grandfather was being urged by his wife Mary Jane to come home, perhaps to salvage what they could of the harvest so that the family could make it through the winter, or simply because, as an older man with a family, he was being reminded of his moral obligation to protect his loved ones, a duty certainly as important in his mind as his duty to fight, especially given the confusion of loyalties that occur in a civil war.

CHOOSING: THE BATTLE OF FRANKLIN
John Donne, 'Valediction Forbidding Mourning'.

General Hood's attempt to outflank Sherman's forces was strategically successful in that the army arrived outside Franklin ahead of the pursuing Federal forces under the command of John M. Schofield, but Hood and his officers celebrated on the evening of November 29th to such an extent that the General was not in control of his powers sufficiently to give the command to attack when the unsuspecting Federal troops marched between the Confederate lines that night. The result was that the Federal troops were allowed to pass unchallenged and to establish an effective defensive perimeter outside Franklin. The ensuing battle the next day decimated the Confederates. Over six thousand troops were lost in what was statistically one of the bloodiest battles of the war.

The battle was only a few miles fom Great Grandfather's small farm, and either at this battle or after the battle of Nashville, he returned home, having travelled in a complete circle since his departure two years before.

PART FOUR
WAITING FOR THE MESSIAH

William Wordsworth, 'Lines: Composed a Few Miles Above Tintern Abbey . . .'

The first seven years of my life were spent in Greensboro, North Carolina, except for one year in Commerce, Georgia during the 1945 polio epidemic. We lived on the outskirts of town beside a large, dense and lovely forest where I spent a good part of my time. The same intimacy with nature which Wordsworth implies in his own recollections I too felt. I still look upon those years, that place, and that time of my life as rarified and full of mystery and insight and magic.

STARMOUNT FOREST PROLOGUE
Dylan Thomas, 'Fern Hill'.

Actually, in the ancient Hebrew model of the universe the earth was conceived of as having the structure of a table top supported by columns in the ocean with a hemispherical barrier above the stars, planets, and sun (the firmament of the sky). Above this were the waters above the firmament, and heaven was above those waters. In my own paradigm, the earth was a globe floating in space with the dirt settled on the bottom.

LA BELLE DAME
Plato, 'Phaedrus', *The Dialogues of Plato*, trans. M.A. Jowett (New York: Random House, 1920), p. 254.

TETHERED CHILD
'Abdu'l-Bahá, *Selections from the Writings of 'Abdu'l-Bahá*, p. 126.

HAMILTON LAKE
'Abdu'l-Bahá, *Foundations of World Unity* (Wilmette, Ill.: Bahá'í Publishing Trust, 1945), p. 9.

WAITING FOR THE MESSIAH
Luke 18:17.

HOUSES
'Uncle McNeill' is Edwin McNeill Poteat, who taught theology in Peking (Beijing) for eleven years before fleeing in 1928 during civil unrest when the National People's Army captured Peking. He returned to the United States where he was a prominent Baptist minister, writing over a dozen books, including a number of poetry volumes published by Harper & Brothers.

NECROMANCY
Virginia Rebecca Southall Hatcher was my grandmother on my father's
side. She was the only grandparent I ever knew.

PART FIVE
A RITE OF PASSAGE

Bahá'u'lláh, *The Seven Valleys and the Four Valleys*. 2nd edition. Translated
by Ali-Kuli Khan and Marzieh Gail (Wilmette, Ill.: Bahá'í Publishing
Trust, 1978), p. 7.

HITCHHIKING THROUGH THE NORTH GEORGIA MOUNTAINS
Sidney Lanier (1842–1881) was a poet and musician born in Georgia.
Given dangerous assignments as a signal officer during the Civil War, he
was captured, was imprisoned, and contracted an illness from which he
never fully recovered. He was a brilliant student of poetry and music (he
was a superb flautist). One of his best known poetic works 'Song of the
Chattachoochee' is a celebration of this beautiful area, which had been
settled in the late 1700s by Scottish trappers who co-existed with the
Cherokee and Creek Indians. It was in this locale that I spent many
summers hiking and camping when I was growing up, but during that
time, this same vicinity was notorious for its moonshiners, racial violence,
and general ill will towards 'outsiders'.

WHATEVER HAPPENED TO JUNGLE JERRY?
The Everglades is a marsh and swamp covering a large area (4,000 square
miles) of southern Florida.

HEMINGWAY'S HOUSE IN KEY WEST
Hemingway, 'The Short Happy Life of Francis Macomber'. *'Ezra . . .'*
Ezra Pound.

ALL I HAVE TO SHOW AFTER CAMPING OUT
Geronimo or Goyakla (1829–1908) was a brave, brilliant, and determined
leader of the Apaches. He was deceived by duplicitous representatives of
the American government and finally captured in Skeleton Canyon in this
same wilderness area on the border between Arizona and New Mexico.
General Crook, who for a time succeeded in establishing peace with the
Indians during the 1870s, is quoted as having stated that in the future, 'we
will decide that Geronimo was one of the greatest "Americans" that ever
lived'. In the Bahá'í Writings, 'Abdu'l-Bahá states that the American
Indians have such potential that, if they are allowed to become educated,
they 'will become so illumined as to enlighten the whole world'. (Quoted
in *Citadel of Faith*, letters by Shoghi Effendi (Wilmette, Ill.: Bahá'í
Publishing Trust, 1965), p. 16.

EL METRO, 1961
'Guerra Civil', the Spanish Civil War (1936–38)

197

LEAVING SPAIN

'*Madrileños*', citizens of Madrid.

'*tranvías*', streetcars.

'*novias*', sweethearts.

'*Guardia Civil*', a sort of military police force assigned primarily to rural areas.

'*El Cantar de Mío Cid*', *The Song of the Cid*, a twelfth-century epic poem about Rodrigo Diaz de Vivar, a hero of Christian Spain who in the 11th century seized control of the Moorish kingdom of Valencia.

'*Castellano*', the distinctive Spanish dialect of the province of Castile.
'*sin acento*', without accent.

'*Valle de los Caídos*', Valley of the Fallen, a memorial statue and cathedral dedicated to the war dead. Built by Franco with slave labor, the memorial was particularly offensive to the Madrid veterans because, among other things, the civilian population of Madrid had been so heartlessly besieged during the war by Franco's Falangist army.

'*El Escorial*', a village in the mountains northwest of Madrid where Philip II built an elaborate monastery in which almost all the Spanish sovereigns are buried. Above the monastery nestled in the mountains is a seat carved from solid rock where legend has it the King was wont to meditate.

'*rejoneador*', fights the bull on horseback using a lance, thus all control of the horse is accomplished with feet and legs.

Completed in 1819, the Prado is one of the finest museums in the world and houses the best collection of Spanish painting.

Planned in the 1550s, the '*Retiro*' park occupies over 300 acres in the city. It has a zoological gardens as well as a variety of other lovely features.

'*mi direcíon*', my address.

'*Alberto Aquilera . . .*', number seven Alberto Aquilera, beneath the archway.

A PILGRIMAGE TO CHRIST'S TOMB

Though archeological evidence rather significantly disputes the claim for Christ's tomb being outside the present walls of Jerusalem, the Protestant belief in this site is understandable given its visual impact.

'*Quem quaeritis*', 'Whom do you seek?' The question asked of the three Marys by the angel when they visit the tomb of Christ. This begins the Easter sepulcher service in the liturgy of the Catholic church and formed the basis for the beginnings of medieval drama which evolved out of these dramatic choral pieces as early as the tenth century. After the Marys respond that they are looking for Christ, they are told He has risen.

A POSTCARD FROM NASSAU

William James (1842–1910), a teacher of philosophy at Harvard along with such other notables as Josiah Royce and George Santayana. James was a proponent of the philosophy of Pragmatism.

'The Duke', the Duke of Windsor who in 1936 abdicated the English throne to marry the twice-divorced Wallis Simpson. After a two-year stay in France, the couple moved to the Bahamas where he was Governor.

PART SIX

WAITING FOR THE PRIME AFTER THE PRIME

Denis de Rougement, *Love in the Western World*, translated from the French by Montgomery Belgion (New York: Fawcett World Library, 1956), p. 22. For me, this remains the most insightful and useful study of the origins and nature of the courtly love conventions in medieval poetry, as well as a thoroughly engaging explanation for most of our contemporary attitudes towards romantic love.

RESCINDING
   Bahá'u'lláh, *The Hidden Words*, p. 11.

THE ALBATROSS AROUND MY NECK
   Delmore Schwartz, 'The Heavy Bear Who Goes With Me'.

WATCHING YOUR WINDOW
   Bahá'u'lláh, *The Seven Valleys*, p. 8.

AUBADE
   An 'aubade' is a song or poem for the morning, though in the lyric mode it has come to connote the parting speeches of lovers when daybreak disrupts their communion.
   'O, swear . . .' the lines preceding the most famous of aubades, the parting speeches between Romeo and Juliet in Act II, scene ii of Shakespeare's play.

YOUR HANDS
   'Petrarch . . .' Petrarch's lyrics to his beloved Laura form the basis for the lyric treatment of idealized love in the Renaissance, and the whole notion of idealized and ultimately unattainable love becomes known as 'Petrarchan'.
   '*Frauendienst*' is difficult to translate, but means something like 'the spirit of woman'; the term designates the attitude toward women in the courtly love tradition: woman is worshipped, idolized, and obeyed, though she is perceived above all else to be more of a sexual object than a human being.

PART SEVEN

TUNNEL VISION

Joseph Campbell, *The Hero with a Thousand Faces* (New York: The World Publishing Company, 1967), p. 337. In his discussion of the paradigm of the

199

archetypal hero in art and literature, Campbell makes this observation about the hero as warrior in his chapter 'Transformations of the Hero'.

DIVORCE II
'The Picasso . . .' The painting being described here is 'Figures by the Sea' (1903).

SUNBATHERS
Dr. John Ott has studied the effects of full spectrum lighting on human health and personality disorders. He came upon his theory while doing time-lapse photography for Walt Disney studios—he discovered that deprivation of certain wave-lengths—particularly ultra-violet light—caused specific retardation in physical growth and demonstrable personality disorders. He observed these first in plants, and then recorded with time-lapse photography the same effects with animals and humans. He has always been most generous in sharing his ideas with me.

The inspiration for this piece occurred when, after having taught at my university in Florida for over ten years, I looked out the window of my office one spring to see the girls sunning themselves. I thought to myself, 'There she is again', before I realized that the girl whom I had first seen in that same spot was now in her thirties.

A MORNING PRAYER
Bahá'u'lláh, 'Words of Wisdom', in *Tablets of Bahá'u'lláh Revealed after the Kitáb-i-Aqdas*. Compiled by the Research Department of the Universal House of Justice. (Haifa: Bahá'í World Centre, 1978), p. 156.

'there would have been . . .' Shakespeare's *Macbeth*, Act V, scene v, l. 18. Macbeth, who awaits attack at his castle, has just been told the queen has died. Immediately afterward he receives message that the forest is moving toward the castle, thus fulfilling the witches' prophecy regarding his own doom.

MY FEARS ABOUT THE AFTERLIFE
Raymond Moody, Jr., *Life After Life* (New York: Bantam, 1975), p. 143. Though Moody's book was first taken to be an indication that all souls receive a uniformly blissful afterlife, he describes, in a little considered alternative to the positive experience, a negative 'limbo' state wherein a sort of penance is accomplished for some sort of violation of life's purposes. According to one subject, 'If you leave here a tormented soul, you will be a tormented soul over there, too.'

'Aunt Cynthia's . . .' Cousin Keebie and I used to hike, hunt, and play in the same fields on which Great Grandfather had fought in the Battle of Franklin (November 30, 1864).

'if John Wesley . . .' After an unsuccessful and dispiriting time as an Anglican missionary to Georgia in the early 1730s, John Wesley returned to England. On May 24, 1738, in Aldersgate Street in London, he experienced a spiritual epiphany at a small meeting of Moravians. This convinced him to abandon the intellectuality of the Church of England

and to promulgate the Pauline concept of justification through grace. John Wesley subsequently founded the Methodist Church.

'Old Man Haver's . . .' Mr. Haver had a small store on Highland Avenue in Atlanta. He would always yell at us and accuse us of stealing things, which naturally prompted us to get back at him by stealing things, particularly twenty-five cent Comet stick-model airplanes (the fifty-cent models were too difficult for us to make).

'Thomas Mitchell . . .' The movie was 'Adventure', a 1945 film with Clark Gable, Greer Garson, and Thomas Mitchell.

PART EIGHT
WAITING FOR AMERICA

'Blessed Exile's . . .' Hayden's poem 'Words in the Mourning Time' alludes here to Bahá'u'lláh, Who was exiled from His native Persia to Iraq, to Constantinople, to Adrianople, and finally to the prison city of Akka (in Israel). He was the Founder of the Bahá'í Faith and enunciated in His writings the Bahá'í belief that the history of religion properly understood is the unfolding of a plan of progressive enlightenment whereby God periodically sends Prophets or Teachers to educate human-kind by degrees. The Bahá'í teachings believe this particular period in history as a crucial point of transition for humanity much as adolescence in the individual signifies the transition from childhood to maturity. From such a perspective, Bahá'ís view the turmoil of our age as the death throes of antiquated concepts of human identity and the birth of a world consciousness—humankind as an organic creation and the earth as one country. However, such longterm optimism does not lessen what Bahá'ís believe will be the pain and suffering resulting from the difficulty of this transition.

DR. WILL AND THE DEATH OF HARMONY GROVE
The information for this portrait of my Grandfather on my mother's side is taken mostly from *Memoirs of Dr. W.B.J. Hardman and Elizabeth Susan Colquitt Hardman and Their Children* by Thomas Colquitt Hardman (Athens, Georgia: The McGregor Company, 1953).

ROY ROGERS CONTEMPLATES IMMORTALITY
When his horse Trigger died, Roy Rogers, the archetypal American cinematic cowboy, had the horse stuffed and mounted.

SIXTEEN SECONDS BETWEEN GROUND ZERO
AND SAMARA DRIVE
'Ground Zero', a term used to designate the point of impact of a nuclear bomb. In grammar school we used to wear 'dog tags' and practice the various positions to assume in the event of a nuclear attack. The nature of our response was supposed to be determined by how far we calculated we

201

were from 'ground zero'. This was around 1948 before anything much about 'fallout' was understood.

MEMO: ATTENTION ARCHEOLOGISTS
'Heinrich Schliemann' retired at the age of 36 with considerable wealth in order to pursue his belief that the Troy of Homer's epic had actually existed. In 1868, having virtually memorized Homer's work, he sailed the coast of Greece and Asia Minor and discovered the site of ancient Troy, as well as many other equally impressive sites. He is generally acknowledged to be the father of modern archeology.

'*beahs*', literally 'bows', though sometimes translated as 'rings', were actually malleable strips of gold (malleable because mostly unalloyed) used as ornamental bracelets, arm bands, etc., but were also accepted as currency, especially in the tribal era prior to the Anglo-Saxon use of forged coins. They are mentioned in the epics as reward to warriors for heroic deeds.

'Sutton Hoo . . .' In 1939 an Anglo-Saxon burial ship was discovered at the Sutton Hoo estate near Woodbridge, Suffolk, containing amazingly rich artefacts, most probably from the burial of a 7th-century East Anglian king. The effect of this find was to demonstrate that the fantastic treasures described in such works as *Beowulf* are not poetic fiction, but the accurate depiction of a very rich culture. Remnants of the harp were indeed found. This discovery totally changed scholarly opinion about the historicity of the Anglo-Saxon heroic poetry and so-called 'folk poetry' in general, particularly works of the oral-formulaic tradition.

BECCA
Theodore Roethke, 'Elegy for Jane'.

Rebecca Dye (1977–1987) was a longtime (six years) ballet student of my wife's who was hit by a car and killed while helping children cross a street as a 'crossing guard'. This occurred on the first day of school, 1987.

'*there was such speed . . .*' These lines are from the poem 'Bells for John Whiteside's Daughter,' by John Crowe Ransom.

'Jane Banks . . .' Two months before the tragedy, Becca had played one of the leads in a production of *Mary Poppins*.

PART NINE
A SENSE OF HISTORY

Bahá'u'lláh, *Gleanings from the Writings of Baha'u'llah*, pp. 12–13.

A SENSE OF HISTORY
Arnold Toynbee, *Christianity Among the Religions of the World* (New York: Charles Scribner's Sons, 1957), p. 104.

'*taqíyyih . . .*' An oral denial of one's faith, allowed by <u>Sh</u>í'ah Islam to believers in times of peril. This law was abrogated by Bahá'u'lláh. Bahá'ís are admonished to obey the law of the land in which they abide, but they cannot recant their beliefs, even if so directed by the authorities.

'Badí' . . .' His name, given him by Bahá'u'lláh, means 'Wonderful'. Badí' was sent by Bahá'u'lláh to deliver His letter to the Shah. Badí' was tortured and killed, his body then buried in an obscure place (Safíd-Áb), but the Bahá'ís discovered the site, which then became a place of pilgrimage. (See H.M. Balyuzi, *Bahá'u'lláh: The King of Glory* (Oxford: George Ronald, 1980), p. 307.

'Rúhu'lláh . . .' 'Varqá' (the Dove) was the title bestowed by Bahá'u'lláh on the Bahá'í teacher and poet Mírzá 'Ali-Muḥammad who in 1896 was stabbed in the belly with a dagger and then cut to pieces in front of his twelve-year-old son Rúhu'lláh. The boy was then asked to recant his beliefs, and upon refusing to do so, he was strangled with a rope.

'Qájár line . . .' The Turkoman tribe who usurped the Persian throne and reigned from 1795–1925.

'a chorus of portraits . . .' In the hallway at the top of the stairs of the entrance to the mansion of Bahjí where Bahá'u'lláh spent the last years of His life, the Guardian of the Bahá'í Faith, Shoghi Effendi, placed on one wall the portrait of the Shah and on the opposite wall the pictures of National Spiritual Assemblies as they formed throughout the world.

THE PRIMAL POINT

The Báb, quoted in *The World Order of Bahá'u'lláh*, (Wilmette, Ill.: Bahá'í Publishing Trust, 1938), p. 126.

Shoghi Effendi, *God Passes By*, p. 7.

For detailed accounts of this declaration of the Bab to Mullá Ḥusayn, see *God Passes By* (pp. 3–7), and Nabíl-i-A'ẓam, *The Dawn-Breakers* (Wilmette, Ill.: Bahá'í Publishing Trust, 1962), chapter III.

'a young Siyyid . . .' Mírzá'Alí-Muḥammad, called the Siyyid-i-Báb by the Persian people, the Báb by His followers. At the time of this event He was twenty-five years old.

'fulfilling . . .' Mullá Ḥusayn had been a follower of Siyyid Káẓim-i-Rashtí, himself a student of the famous Shaykh-Aḥmad-i-Aḥsa'í, both of whom had taught that the time for the promised Qá'im had come. At the death of Siyyid Káẓim in December of 1843, Mullá Ḥusayn set out to search for the Promised One, having in his own mind as a final test for anyone he might find worthy—that such a one would, unasked, reveal the meaning of the difficult Surih of Joseph from the Qur'án. This the Báb did, revealing without stopping in the course of that fateful evening the Surih of Mulk of the *Qayyúmu'l-Asmá'*, the Báb's commentary on the Surih of Joseph. In this work the Báb explains that the figure of Joseph is symbolic of the Manifestation (Bahá'u'lláh) for whom the whole world is searching. Like Joseph, Bahá'u'lláh's own brother (Mírzá Yaḥyá, Ṣubḥ-i-Azal) caused him great sorrow, even attempting on several occasions to have Bahá'u'lláh killed.

'adhán . . .' Literally 'announcement', though designating here the morning call to prayer.

MULLÁ ḤUSAYN

'Kaziran gate . . .' the gate to the city of Shiraz near the spot where Mullá Ḥusayn first encountered the Báb.

'Bábu'l-Báb', the 'Gate unto the Gate', a title given Mullá Ḥusayn by the Báb because Mullá Ḥusayn was the first to believe in Him.

'priestly titles', Mullá Ḥusayn was a respected theologian and Muslim scholar.

'long trek . . .' Mullá Ḥusayn was immediately given the mission of taking an epistle to an unknown recipient in Tehran—to whomever he discovered to be worthy. Mullá Ḥusayn made this lengthy journey on foot, and in Tehran met and gave the Tablet to Mírzá Ḥusayn-'Alí (Bahá'u'lláh).

'Bábíyyih', the house of Mírzá Muḥammad-Báqir-i-Qá'iní, which acquired this title because it was always open to anyone wishing to meet Mullá Ḥusayn and learn about the Báb. After delivering the letter to Bahá'u'lláh, Mullá Ḥusayn travelled to his native Mashhad where he taught the new Faith to all who would listen.

'fort Ṭabarsí'. Mullá Ḥusayn's life ended as he and a handful of Bábís defended themselves against government troops in the hastily devised fort they made at the Shrine of Shaykh Ṭabarsí near the village of Sárí. During this extended siege, Mullá Ḥusayn, but a student and small in stature, became a scourge to the attacking soldiers, at one point delivering a blow with his sword which severed in two a soldier, his rifle, and the tree behind which he stood. As a result of his heroism, Mullá Ḥusayn's ferocious courage has come to symbolize for Bahá'ís the spirit of the early believers during the Heroic Age of the Bahá'í Faith (1844–1921).

THE GARDENS OF BADASHT

According to the account of Shoghi Effendi in *God Passes By*, a conference was called by Bahá'u'lláh (in consultation with the Báb) ostensibly to plan how to free the Báb from imprisonment, but in reality to mark the Bábí Faith as a new and separate religion. To accomplish this, Bahá'u'lláh planned with Quddus and Ṭáhirih to act out this break, with Quddus representing the conservative element among the believers who wished to remain Muslim, and Ṭáhirih espousing the view that the religion of the Báb represented a completely new stage in religious history.

"Abdu'l-Kháliq', as a faithful Moslem, was so devastated at seeing Ṭáhirih unveiled, thus breaching a most fundamental social tenet of Islam, that he cut his own throat, though he survived the wound.

IN HIS NAME, THE CONCEALER

Bahá'u'lláh, *Kitáb-i-Íqán: The Book of Certitude*. Translated by Shoghi Effendi (Wilmette, Ill.: Bahá'í Publishing Trust, 1950), p. 4. Part of the opening statement by Bahá'u'lláh in this treatise on the Divine plan of God, these words describe forthrightly the irony of human history—that whenever God sends divine assistance in the form of the Prophets, the human race almost inevitably rejects and persecutes these benign teachers.

The setting here is the execution of the Báb in the city of Tabríz. The events alluded to are thoroughly documented by Bahá'í and non-Bahá'í sources (see *God Passes By*, pp. 49–60 and *The Dawn Breakers*, pp. 500–526).

'ghostly Greek . . .' Socrates in Plato's dialogue 'The Gorgias'.

'crowds gather . . .' About ten thousand people witnessed these events.

'what tricks . . .' When the guards came to get the Báb, He had not yet finished dictating His final instructions to His amanuensis. He warned the guards that no power could thwart His completion of this task, but the guards took Him and the young Anís, suspended them in the barracks square, and prepared for the execution. Three files of two hundred and fifty men each opened fire in turn. When the smoke cleared, the Báb had disappeared, though the ropes which had suspended him hung there severed by the bullets. He was found unharmed shortly afterward completing His instructions.

'Náṣirí soldiers . . .' The actual execution was carried out by the Náṣirí bodyguard because the 'grieving Christian colonel' (Sám <u>Kh</u>án, a Christian officer of the Armenian regiment) had refused to carry out the orders a second time—the Báb had told him that if he was sincere in his desire not to carry out the execution, God would relieve him of his 'perplexity'.

'The day will come', quoted in *God Passes By*, p. 53.

'bitter taste of hemlock . . .' Socrates was executed by being given a draught of poison hemlock to drink, his penalty for teaching such things as the doctrine of monotheism, which the state felt dangerous.

ṬÁHIRIH

Ṭáhirih spoke these words to the wife of the Kalantar in whose house she was confined immediately before her execution; quoted in *The Dawn Breakers*, p. 622.

'I held/ the infant Master . . .' See 'Abdu'l-Bahá, *Memorials of the Faithful*, translated by Marzieh Gail (Wilmette, Ill.: Bahá'í Publishing Trust, 1971), p. 200. Ṭáhirih held the young 'Abdu'l-Bahá on her lap as she said to the scholarly Vaḥíd, 'Let deeds, not words, testify to thy faith, if thou art a man of true learning.'

'dangling my colors . . .' When the headsmen refused to excute her according to the imperial farman, a 'slave was found, far gone in drunkenness; besotted, vicious, black of heart. And he strangled Ṭáhirih. He forced a scarf between her lips and rammed it down her throat.' 'Abdu'l-Bahá, *Memorials of the Faithful*, p. 203. The kerchief used was one she herself chose and wore around her neck for the occasion. (See *The Dawn-Breakers*, p. 626, and *God Passes By*, p. 75.

'the emancipation/ of us all . . .' At her death Ṭáhirih declared, 'You can kill me as soon as you like, but you cannot stop the emancipation of women.' (quoted in *God Passes By*, p. 75.

ṢUBḤ-I-AZAL

In the dialogue 'The Gorgias', *Plato's Gorgias*, trans. W. C. Helmbold (New York: Liberal Arts Press, 1955), p. 40.

'Ṣubḥ-i-Azal', the title of Bahá'u'lláh's half-brother Mírzá Yaḥyá, means 'Morning of Eternity'. Though designated by the Báb to guide the Bábí community, Yaḥyá was so consumed with jealousy and fear that he tried to kill Bahá'u'lláh (and very nearly succeeded). When all else failed, he tried to convince the government officials in Adrianople that Bahá'u'lláh was a trouble-maker. The plot backfired when the government solved the problem by exiling all the so-called Bábís, sending Mírzá Yaḥyá himself in exile to Famagusta in Cyprus where his personal influence on the religion was effectively ended.

THE MOST GREAT PRISON

Bahá'u'lláh called the barracks in Akka 'The Most Great Prison', stating the following: 'Know thou that upon Our arrival at this Spot, We chose to designate it as the "Most Great Prison." Though previously subjected in another land (Tehran) to chains and fetters, We yet refused to call it by that name. Say: Ponder thereon, O yet endued with understanding!' (quoted in *God Passes By*, p. 185.)

SEVEN PICTURES OF THE MASTER

'Abdu'l-Bahá, quoted in *The Mystery of God* (New Delhi, India: Bahá'í Publishing Trust, 1971), p. 22. 'Abdu'l-Bahá's given name was Abbas Effendi and Bahá'u'lláh bestowed on him several lofty titles befitting his station: *Áqá* (Master), Sirru'lláh (Mystery of God), and *Ghuṣn-i-A'ẓam* (the Most Great Branch). He chose for himself the title *'Abdu'l-Bahá* (Servant of the Glory) to demonstrate that he in no wise considered himself to be co-equal with the Manifestation of God.

1853

When an attempt was made on the life of the Shah, Bahá'u'lláh was imprisoned along with other Bábís. They were placed in the infamous Siy'áh-Chál dungeon, the Black Pit in the slums of Tehran, their feet in stocks, their necks strung together by the Qará-Guhar chain. It was during this period that Bahá'u'lláh received the first intimations of His revelation. On one notable occasion, 'Abdu'l-Bahá came to visit his Father. The full account of this incident is discussed in H.M. Balyuzi, *'Abdu'l-Bahá: The Centre of the Covenant of Bahá'u'lláh* (London: George Ronald, 1971), pp. 11–12.

'who has heard . . .' 'Abdu'l-Bahá was the first to believe in His Father's station as a Prophet of God.

1892

Hand of the Cause of God Ṭarázu'lláh Samandarí (1874–1968). For a complete description of this event, see *The Bahá'í World: An International Record*, Vol XV, 1968–1973 (Haifa, Israel: Bahá'í World Centre, 1976), pp. 411–412.

1899

'Abdu'l-Bahá was called 'Father of the Poor' because he would give gifts of money or food and clothing to the impoverished people in Akka and Haifa. He was later knighted by the British government for the help He gave to the people of Palestine during the First World War.

'Look at me . . .' These words were spoken by 'Abdu'l-Bahá to one of the first groups of pilgrims from the West that visited him in 1898–99. Quoted in *An Early Pilgrimage* by May Maxwell (London: George Ronald, 1970), p. 42. Some of these pilgrims became the most stalwart teachers of the Bahá'í Faith throughout the world.

1909

This scene takes place on Mount Carmel on the evening when the remains of the Báb, having been carefully hidden by Bahá'ís for 56 years, were at last entombed in the Shrine of the Báb. The prophecy is Zechariah 6:12: 'Thus speaketh the Lord of hosts, saying, Behold the man whose name is The Branch; and he shall grow up out of his place, and he shall build the temple of the Lord.' For a complete description of this event, see H.M. Balyuzi, *'Abdu'l-Bahá*, pp. 126–130.

1913

During his visit to America (1912–13), 'Abdu'l-Bahá devoted his time to visiting the Bahá'ís in the various communities across the United States and on occasion giving talks about the Bahá'í Faith. On April 19, 1912, he spoke at the Bowery Mission. The full text of that talk appears in *The Promulgation of Universal Peace: Talks Delivered by 'Abdu'l-Bahá during His Visit to the United States and Canada in* 1912, compiled by Howard MacNutt (Wilmette, Ill.: Bahá'í Publishing Trust, 1982), pp. 32–34.

1916

'Himself fleshing out . . .' Another of his titles was 'Exemplar', and in this capacity he is described by the Guardian of the Bahá'í Faith as having a station unique in the annals of religious history (see *God Passes By*, pp. 242–243).

1921

Bahá'u'lláh had taken 'Abdu'l-Bahá to Mount Carmel and designated for him the spot where the Shrine of the Báb was to be built. This spot is believed by Bahá'ís to be the pivotal point of the coming world civilization in that the arc of buildings surrounding this point will function as the headquarters of the Universal House of Justice and the repository of the Writings of Bahá'u'lláh. Shoghi Effendi describes the symbolic significance of this site in *Citadel of Faith*, pp. 95–96.

'Now it is finished . . .' some of the last words of 'Abdu'l-Bahá, quoted in H.M. Balyuzi, *'Abdu'l-Bahá*, p. 460.

'a youthful branch . . .' In his *Will and Testament*, 'Abdu'l-Bahá used these phrases in appointing Shoghi Effendi Guardian of the Bahá'í Faith.

ST PAUL'S VISIT TO ALBERT SCHWEITZER'S JUNGLE MISSION
Ṭáhirih quoted in *Memorials of the Faithful*, p. 200.

'none of these things . . .' The left part of this poem was taken verbatim from a religious tract left on my car windshield in Nashville, Tennessee in 1963, though the Pauline sense of it complies with much so-called fundamentalist Christian theology.

'the dissertation . . .' Schweitzer gave up his prominence as an organist, theologian and physician to minister to the sick in Africa (beginning in 1913). His dissertation *The Quest for the Historical Jesus* was part of his overall investigation of Christian theology and his ultimate determination to forgo all that the world might bestow on him for all his genius, and to follow what he believed to be the example Christ himself established and described. This very existential response to his Christian belief seems markedly at odds with Pauline Christianity. His problem with Paul's theology is discussed at length in his autobiographical work *Out of My Life and Thought*.

THE LOTUS OF BAHAPOUR
The Tablet of Carmel, *Gleanings from the Writings of Bahá'u'lláh*, p. 16.

The building of the lotus-shaped Bahá'í Temple (*Mashriqu'l-Adhkár*, 'Dawning-place of the Mention of God', outside New Delhi was completed in 1986. The steel structure of the building is covered entirely with sheets of white marble.

'Sulaymán Khán . . .' Sulaymán Khán-i-Tunukábání, also known as Jamálu'd-Dín, an early teacher of the Faith sent by Bahá'u'lláh to India and responsible for much of the rapid growth of the Bahá'í Faith that later took place there.

'Bolivian jungle villages . . .' An ongoing teaching project in Bolivia has resulted in the establishment of a Baha'í radio station and school in which children are taught to read and write. In many of these villages, both in India and Bolivia, the village government itself is run according to the principles of Bahá'í administration.

'in the Dakotas . . .' Many prophecies of the American Indians seem to allude to this period in history and to the Bahá'í Faith. For this reason, the Faith is presently growing rapidly among various Indian tribes.

SUNBURST
Bahá'u'lláh, *Gleanings*, pp. 12–13.

CORRESPONDENCES
'Abdu'l-Bahá, *Selections*, p. 178.

This title parallels the title of a poem by Charles Baudelaire and deals with the same essential theme. The setting is an almost perfect circle of Sequoa at Bosch Bahá'í School located in the mountains above Santa Cruz, California.

'Abdu'l-Bahá, *Selections*, p. 178.

'quakes and flames . . .' The San Francisco earthquake of 1906. The city was quickly rebuilt between 1906 and 1910.

'She hath deceived . . .', *Othello*, Act I, scene iii, L. 294.

GREEN LAKE, WISCONSIN

Rúmí (1207–1273), the most famous Persian Sufi poet.

Bahá'ís have held annual Green Lake Conference for about thirty years at the conference center owned by the American Baptist Assembly in Green Lake, Wisconsin. The beginnings of the center stem from the summer of 1888 when Mrs. Victor Lawson of Chicago took friends for a boat ride on Green Lake. When a sudden storm caused them to put in at Lone Tree Point, Mrs. Lawson saw the potential there and before the year was out had purchased ten acres, to which much more was added by the family in the years to come.

'John Wesley . . .'. see the note to 'My Fears about the Afterlife.'

'Ulysses . . .', see the note to Foreknowledge and the True Story of Marvin Rainwater's Remarkable Vision.

'a new race . . .' In *The Advent of Divine Justice* (Wilmette, Ill.: Bahá'í Publishing Trust, 1956), p. 14, Shoghi Effendi states that the 'distinguishing function' of Bahá'u'lláh's Revelation is 'none other than the calling into being of a new race of men.' He further quotes Bahá'u'lláh as stating that 'A race of men, incomparable in character, shall be raised up which, with the feet of detachment, will tread under all who are in heaven and on earth, and will cast the sleeve of holiness over all that hath been created from water and clay.' (p. 26).